Charcuterie Boards Cookbook

Master the Art of Stunning and Flavorful Charcuterie Arrangements for Every Occasion [III EDITION]

Sarah Roslin

TABLE OF CONTENTS

1 INTRODUCTION

Charcuterie boards are a delightful assembly of cured meats, cheeses, artisan breads, olives, fruits, nuts, and various accompaniments, arranged creatively on a platter, designed to cater to a wide array of palates. They are a centerpiece for gatherings, an icebreaker for conversations, and a canvas for culinary artistry. Not just a means to satiate hunger, charcuterie boards are a social experience, shared and savored amongst friends, family, and food enthusiasts alike.

Dive into the delightful world of dicing, slicing, and artful arranging with our "Charcuterie Board Cookbook"! This isn't just about slapping salami on a slab of wood. Oh no! It's about creating stories and experiences that dance across the palate. Here, you'll discover the secrets to crafting the perfect balance of flavors, textures, and aesthetics that transform simple gatherings into unforgettable feasts. From the zing of artisanal mustard to the richness of aged cheddar, let each page guide you through a journey that celebrates the timeless tradition of communal indulgence. So, grab your knives and boards—adventure wait in every slice!

1.1 History of Charcuterie Boards

The United States:

During the 19th and 20th centuries, dinner party dishes in the United States underwent changes. In the 1910s, cocktail parties featuring finger foods became popular. As interest in European cuisine grew during World War II, dishes from France, Italy, Germany, and Greece gained popularity among Americans. In the 1990s, American supermarkets started offering a wider range of products, coinciding with the rise in popularity of charcuterie boards. Today, charcuterie boards are not only a part of the starter menu in restaurants but are also served at home dinner parties. They are simple to prepare and serve, making them a popular choice. In the era of social media, charcuterie boards have gained fame, with different styles of these boards circulating on various platforms. People share pictures of their charcuterie boards, attracting attention from others. In 2019, an American company reported that sales of charcuterie board-style meat lunches reached $561 million, an 8.1% increase from the previous year.

Europe:

The term "charcuterie" originated in 15th-century France and refers to cured meat. The word comes from the French words "chair" (flesh) and "cut" (cooked). The establishment of charcuterie stores in France, known as "charcuteries," contributed to the development of stylized food serving and decoration in French cuisine.

Food historian Sarah Wassberg Johnson asserts that charcuterie also has its roots in the plain foods consumed by European laborers since the Middle Ages. Their meals consisted of meats, cheeses, bread, and wine. Over time, these meals gained popularity among the upper class, who added a cheese course to their formal dinners during the 18th and 19th centuries in France, Britain, and colonized America. Cheese remained an integral part of dinner until the late 19th century when it was replaced by the dessert course.

1.2 Composition of Charcuterie Boards

A charcuterie board is traditionally composed of the following elements:

1. **Cured Meats:** Various selections like prosciutto, salami, chorizo, and coppa are staples.
2. **Cheeses:** A mix of hard, soft, aged, and fresh cheeses provides contrast in flavor and texture.
3. **Bread and Crackers:** Sliced baguette, artisan bread, and a variety of crackers serve as vehicles for toppings.
4. **Fruits and Nuts:** Fresh and dried fruits alongside almonds, walnuts, or pecans offer sweetness and crunch.
5. **Pickles and Olives:** Cornichons, pickled onions, or olives add a briny, tangy component.

6. **Spreads and Dips:** Mustards, honey, fruit preserves, or hummus for slathering and dipping.
7. **Garnishes:** Fresh herbs or edible flowers for a pop of color and freshness.

The key to a great charcuterie board lies in the variety and balance of flavors and textures, encouraging guests to create their own perfect bite.

1.3 Varieties of Charcuterie Boards

Charcuterie boards come in various assortments, often themed or tailored to specific tastes, occasions, or culinary traditions. Here are some popular varieties:

1. **Classic French Charcuterie Board:** Focuses on traditional French meats like saucisson, pâté, and ham, paired with Brie, Camembert, or Roquefort cheese, cornichons, and Dijon mustard.
2. **Italian Antipasto Platter:** Includes Italian meats such as prosciutto di Parma, mortadella, and soppressata, alongside cheeses like mozzarella, provolone, and Parmesan, complemented by marinated vegetables and olives.
3. **Spanish Tapas Board:** Features Iberico ham, chorizo, and lomo, coupled with Manchego cheese, marcona almonds, and a selection of olives, often served with slices of crusty bread and aioli.
4. **Mediterranean Mezze Platter:** Offers a colorful spread of hummus, baba ganoush, dolmas (stuffed grape leaves), feta cheese, along with cured meats and flatbreads for dipping.
5. **All-American Board:** Boasts a variety of domestic artisanal meats and cheeses, such as smoked brisket, turkey pastrami, or Vermont cheddar, and could include accompaniments like apple slices, nuts, and a sweet and spicy barbecue sauce.
6. **Vegetarian Charcuterie Board:** Skips the meats and focuses on an abundance of cheeses, roasted vegetables, fruit, nuts, and various dips like guacamole or beet hummus.
7. **Seafood Charcuterie Board:** Swaps out traditional meats for seafood options like smoked salmon, shrimp, tuna tartare, or seafood pâté, paired with appropriate sauces and lemon wedges.
8. **Breakfast/Brunch Board:** Features breakfast meats like bacon and sausages, mini quiches, assorted cheeses, fresh fruits, and breads or pastries.
9. **Dessert Charcuterie Board:** Filled with sweet treats like chocolate, fruits, nuts, mini pastries, and dessert cheeses like mascarpone or cream cheese spreads.
10. **Holiday-Specific Boards:** Tailored for holidays with seasonal items; for example, a Christmas board might feature cranberry-studded cheeses, spiced meats, and gingerbread, while a Halloween board might play with spooky-themed foods.

The beauty of charcuterie boards lies in their versatility and adaptability to different dietary preferences and creative themes. Each board can be customized to the occasion, reflecting the season, the event's theme, or the unique tastes of the guests.

2 THE CHARCUTERIE CRAFTS

2.1 Essential Tools for Brilliance Boards

Creating a charcuterie board requires a set of tools that help in preparation, display, and serving. Here's a list of essential tools for assembling a charcuterie board:

1. **Cutting Boards/Platters:** The base of your display. A large wooden cutting board, marble slab, or a slate board serves as an attractive foundation for arranging your charcuterie spread.
2. **Cheese Knives and Spreaders:** Specialized knives for different types of cheeses — a soft cheese knife, a cheese plane for shaving, a chisel knife for crumbly cheese, and spreaders for soft cheeses and spreads.
3. **Meat Slicer or Sharp Knife:** A sharp chef's knife or a deli slicer for cutting meats thinly and evenly, which is especially important for harder cured meats.

4. **Mandoline Slicer:** For thinly slicing fruits and vegetables consistently, which can be used as garnishes or crisp accompaniments.
5. **Small Bowls or Ramekins:** For holding olives, nuts, dips, and spreads to prevent them from rolling off the board and to keep the presentation tidy.
6. **Toothpicks or Small Forks:** For easy serving and sampling without the need for guests to touch the food directly.
7. **Parchment Paper or Food-Grade Wax Paper:** To line the board for easy cleanup or to separate different foods if desired.
8. **Serving Utensils:** Tongs, small forks, and spoons for guests to serve themselves items like olives, pickles, and spreads without using their hands.
9. **Labels or Place Cards:** To identify the different meats, cheeses, and other items on the board, which is especially helpful for guests with dietary restrictions or preferences.
10. **Food Storage Containers:** For prepping and storing cut meats and cheeses in the refrigerator before assembling the board, as well as for saving leftovers.

2.2 The Charcuterie Choreography: Mastering the Dance of Delightful Display

Arranging a charcuterie board is an artful process that combines aesthetics with practicality, aiming to create an inviting and accessible display that encourages guests to dive in. Here is a step-by-step guide to arranging a charcuterie board:

1. **Choose Your Board:** Select a board that is the right size for your gathering. Wooden boards, slate slabs, or marble trays can all serve as excellent backdrops for your ingredients.
2. **Start with Large Items:** Place any bowls or ramekins that will hold olives, dips, or spreads on the board first. Distributing them evenly will help balance the board and create anchor points for arranging other items.
3. **Add the Cheeses:** Position cheeses next, spacing them out. Consider different shapes and textures — a wedge, a wheel, a chunk — to add visual interest. Cut some pieces to start off, suggesting to guests that it's ready to be enjoyed.
4. **Arrange the Meats:** Fold thin slices of meats like prosciutto into halves or quarters for easy picking. For harder meats like salami, you can make small stacks or fan them out. Space them around the cheeses.
5. **Place Bread and Crackers:** Tuck various breads and crackers in available spaces, ideally near the cheeses and spreads they complement. Some can be in lines, some stacked, or fanned out for an elegant look.
6. **Add Fruits and Vegetables:** Fill in gaps with color — sliced fresh fruits, bunches of grapes, or neatly arranged vegetables can add brightness and balance.
7. **Include Nuts and Dried Fruits:** Sprinkle these in small clusters or along the edges of the board to fill in any small spaces left and to add contrasting textures.
8. **Garnish:** Use fresh herbs, edible flowers, or other garnishes to add a final touch of color and freshness. They can also be used to separate different items or groups.
9. **Ensure Accessibility:** Make sure that every item on the board is easily reachable and that guests won't have to move other items out of the way to get what they want.
10. **Final Touches:** Add serving utensils, cheese knives, and spreaders where needed. If anything needs a drizzle (like honey on cheese), now is the time to add that flourish.
11. **Flow and Abundance:** Aim for a look of abundance. Items should flow into each other and give the sense that there's plenty to go around, without being overcrowded.
12. **Contrast and Space:** Play with contrasts in color, shape, and texture to make the board visually appealing. At the same time, leave a little space around items so guests can identify and pick them up easily.

Remember, the goal is not only to create a board that is visually appealing but also one that invites guests to mix and match flavors and textures to their own tastes. A well-arranged board encourages conversation and interaction as much as it satisfies hunger.

2.3 Charcuterie Palette: A Spectrum of Savory to Sweet

A charcuterie board is a delightful tableau of palate-pleasing foods, each selected for its unique flavor, texture, and ability to complement the other offerings. Here's a breakdown of the types of food typically found on a charcuterie board, along with their varieties:

Cured and Cooked Meats

1. **Prosciutto:** An Italian dry-cured ham that is usually thinly sliced.
2. **Salami:** Available in various styles, such as Genoa, soppressata, and chorizo.
3. **Chorizo:** A spicy Spanish or Mexican pork sausage.
4. **Bresaola:** Air-dried, salted beef that has been aged two or three months until it becomes hard and turns a dark red.
5. **Pâté:** A spreadable paste made from seasoned ground meat and fat, sometimes encased in pastry or set in a mold.
6. **Capicola/Coppa:** Dry-cured pork shoulder or neck.
7. **Mortadella:** A large Italian sausage or luncheon meat made of finely hashed or ground, heat-cured pork.

Cheeses

1. **Soft Cheeses:** Brie, Camembert, goat cheese (chevre), or triple creams.
2. **Semi-Soft Cheeses:** Havarti, Munster, or Port Salut.
3. **Firm Cheeses:** Cheddar, Gouda, Manchego, or Swiss varieties.
4. **Hard Cheeses:** Parmigiano-Reggiano, Pecorino Romano, or aged Gouda.
5. **Blue Cheeses:** Gorgonzola, Roquefort, or Stilton.

Bread and Crackers

1. **Artisan Breads:** Baguette slices, ciabatta, or focaccia.
2. **Crackers:** Water biscuits, seeded crackers, crispbreads, or breadsticks.
3. **Toasts:** Melba toasts or crostini.

Fruits and Nuts

1. **Fresh Fruits:** Grapes, figs, apple slices, pear slices, berries, or melon.
2. **Dried Fruits:** Apricots, figs, dates, or raisins.
3. **Nuts:** Almonds, walnuts, pecans, or pistachios.

Pickles and Olives

1. **Pickles:** Cornichons, gherkins, or pickled onions.
2. **Olives:** Kalamata, green, stuffed, or Castel Vatrano olives.

Spreads and Dips

1. **Mustards:** Dijon, whole grain, or flavored varieties.
2. **Honey:** Natural or infused with flavors like lavender or truffle.
3. **Fruit Preserves:** Fig jam, apricot preserves, or cherry chutney.
4. **Hummus or Tapenades:** Chickpea spread, olive tapenade, or artichoke dip.

Garnishes

1. **Herbs:** Rosemary sprigs, thyme, or basil for a fresh aroma and aesthetic appeal.
2. **Edible Flowers:** Such as nasturtiums or violets for a pop of color.

Others

1. **Chocolate:** Dark, milk, or with nuts and fruits for a sweet contrast.

2. **Seafood:** Smoked salmon, anchovies, or seafood pâté for a piscatorial twist.

This diverse array of foods allows for endless creativity in crafting a charcuterie board. Each item can be chosen to match a specific theme, complement a drink selection, or cater to the dietary preferences and restrictions of your guests.

2.4 Slice of Elegance: The Charcuterie Board Carving Guide

The art of assembling a charcuterie board is complemented by the skill of slicing its components to enhance their flavor and appearance. Different foods call for different slicing techniques, and mastering these can elevate the overall experience of enjoying a charcuterie board.

Meat Slicing Techniques

1. **Thin Slicing for Cured Meats:** Meats like prosciutto and bresaola should be sliced paper-thin to allow their delicate textures and flavors to shine. Use a sharp slicing knife or a meat slicer for consistent, nearly translucent slices.
2. **Chiffonade for Salami:** For salami and other similar sausages, consider a chiffonade cut — rolling the slices into a tube and then slicing them to create ribbons — which makes for easier picking and a more attractive presentation.
3. **Angled Slices for Pâté:** For a pâté or terrine, an angled slice helps to create a larger surface area, which is aesthetically pleasing and makes it easier to spread.

Cheese Slicing Techniques

1. **Wedges for Hard Cheeses:** Hard cheeses like Parmigiano-Reggiano should be broken into small, irregular wedges with a cheese knife to expose their crystalline texture.
2. **Slices for Firm Cheeses:** Firm cheeses such as cheddar or Gouda can be sliced into thin rectangles or squares, making them easy to stack and layer on crackers or bread.
3. **Spreadable for Soft Cheeses:** Soft cheeses, like Brie or Camembert, can be served in wedges or as an entire wheel with a cheese spreader so that guests can scoop their desired amount.

Fruit Slicing Techniques

1. **Wedges for Apples and Pears:** Slice apples and pears into wedges, removing the core, and consider soaking them in lemon water briefly to prevent browning.
2. **Whole or Halved for Grapes:** Grapes can be left whole or sliced in half (especially larger varieties), often kept on the vine for a rustic look.
3. **Slices or Rounds for Citrus:** Citrus fruits, if included, are best in thin rounds or wedges, showcasing their vibrant cross-section.

Vegetable Slicing Techniques

1. **Sticks or Batons for Crunchy Vegetables:** Vegetables like carrots or cucumbers can be cut into sticks or batons for easy dipping and snacking.
2. **Florets for Broccoli or Cauliflower:** These can be broken into small florets to be more bite-sized and manageable.

Bread and Cracker Techniques

1. **Diagonal Slices for Baguettes:** Slice baguette bread diagonally to create elongated pieces that are perfect for topping with cheese and meats.
2. **Rectangular or Triangular Slices for Toast:** When toasting bread, slice it into rectangles or triangles to create more surface area for building bites.

Knowing how to slice each element properly not only affects the texture and taste but also the overall visual appeal of the charcuterie board, making it as much a feast for the eyes as for the palate.

3 FAQ

What are some pro tips for a good charcuterie board?

For a standout charcuterie board, balance flavors from savory to sweet and textures from crunchy to creamy. Use quality, varied meats and cheeses, add colorful produce, offer gluten-free and vegan options, and arrange with accessibility in mind. Serve cheeses at room temperature and meats cool, with condiments for personalized touches.

How much should I serve per person?

Aim for about 2 ounces of meat and cheese per person for an appetizer portion.

Can I include fish on a charcuterie board?

Absolutely. Smoked salmon or cured fish can be a delightful addition.

Should I serve the meats and cheeses at room temperature?

Yes, allowing them to sit at room temperature for about 30 minutes before serving enhances their flavors.

What kind of board should I use?

Wooden, slate, or marble boards are popular, but any flat platter will do.

How should I cut the cheese for a charcuterie board?

It varies. Hard cheeses can be sliced, soft cheeses can be spread, and some can be served in wedges.

Can I make a vegetarian charcuterie board?

Yes, use a variety of cheeses, vegetarian spreads, and plant-based meats.

How do I keep the board from looking too cluttered?

Arrange larger items first and fill in with smaller items, maintaining distinct sections for each type.

How long can a charcuterie board sit out?

It should not sit out for more than 2 hours for food safety reasons.

What's the best way to arrange meats on a charcuterie board?

Fold or roll thin slices, fan out thicker cuts, and stack or spiral others for variety.

How can I accommodate guests with food allergies?

Label all foods and include separate utensils for each item to avoid cross-contamination.

Are there any rules for pairing meats and cheeses?

Pair based on complementary flavors, like mild with mild or bold with bold, but feel free to experiment.

What fruits work best on a charcuterie board?

Grapes, figs, sliced pears, and berries are classic choices.

Should I include something sweet on my charcuterie board?

Yes, chocolates, sweet jams, or honey pair well with salty meats and cheeses.

How do I select the best meats for my board?

Choose a variety of textures and flavors, from delicate to robust.

What kind of bread should I serve?

Offer a selection, such as sliced baguette, artisanal loaves, or crispy breadsticks.

How can I make my charcuterie board stand out?

Use fresh herbs, edible flowers, and interesting containers for a visually appealing display.

Can I prepare a charcuterie board ahead of time?

Partially. Assemble elements that won't dry out or lose texture, and add the rest just before serving.

What drinks pair well with a charcuterie board?

Wine is a classic choice, but craft beers or non-alcoholic sparkling beverages also pair nicely.

Do I need special knives for the board?
Cheese knives and spreaders are helpful but not essential.
What's the best way to serve spreads and dips?
In small bowls with spoons or knives for easy spreading.
How can I keep sliced apples and pears from browning?
Toss them in lemon juice or ascorbic acid solution.
Can a charcuterie board serve as a main course?
Yes, increase the portion sizes and add more substantial items like patés, terrines, or small sandwiches.
What is the etiquette for guests when eating from a charcuterie board?
Use the utensils provided, and avoid double-dipping or touching other foods when selecting items.

COLOR IMAGES:

In your charcuterie boards culinary journey, accuracy is essential. This cookbook provides detailed recipes and, to enhance your cooking experience, we've also curated a high-definition digital collection of color photographs showcasing each dish. To keep the cookbook affordable, these photos are not included in the print version. Instead, they are available in a convenient PDF format, perfectly optimized for your smartphone or tablet. No need for email sign-up. Simply follow the link provided or scan the QR code below. This allows you to view, zoom in, and download these images for offline use, making your plant-based cooking both easier and more enjoyable. We hope this digital resource enriches your experience and helps you unlock the full potential of plant-based cuisine. Happy Cooking!

LINK: https://dl.bookfunnel.com/i69kqjvkiy

4 MIX CHARCUTERIE BOARDS

4.1 Charcuterie board loaded with rosemary, fresh figs, and honey drizzle.

Preparation time: 15 mins |
Cooking time: 0 mins | Servings: 5

Ingredients

- Honey, 1-½ tbsp (22g)
- Cream cheese, 4 oz (120g)
- Cheddar cheese, 4 oz (112g)
- Creamy blue cheese, 4 oz (120g)
- Fresh figs, 4 halves
- Black pepper, as needed.
- Fresh rosemary, as needed.
- Almonds, pumpkin seeds, and food preserves, as needed.

Procedure

1. Mix thoroughly black pepper and honey in a bowl. Place it in one corner of the board.
2. Arrange figs and cheese as you like.
3. Place the cheese slice on the edges pointing outward.
4. Spread nuts and seeds in spare areas.
5. Add fruit preserves in a separate bowl and place them on the board in a corner.
6. Garnish with fresh rosemary.

Nutrition per Serving:

Calories: 260 | Fat: 16g | Carbohydrates: 13g | Protein: 14g | Sugar: 12g | Fiber: 2g | Potassium: 321mg | Sodium: 250mg | Cholesterol: 30mg

4.2 Appetizer Board

Preparation time: 15 mins |
Cooking time: 0 mins | Servings: 3

Ingredients

- Hot Sopressata Salumi, 1 cup (230g)
- Hot Sausage, 4-5
- Italian Herb Sausage, 4-5
- Olives Gigantes, 1 cup (250g)
- Calamata Olives, 1 cup (250g)
- Different types of cheese slices
- Green pitted olives, 1 cup (250g)
- Grissini breadsticks, 2 cups (450g)
- Pistachios, 1 cup (250g)
- Dried apricots, 1 cup (250g)
- Dried apples, 1 cup (250g)
- Dried cranberries, 1 cup (250g)
- Dates, 1 cup (250g)
- Tomato Bruschetta, as needed.
- Assorted Crackers, 1 cup (250g)
- Sesame cashews, 1 cup (250g)

Procedure

1. Arrange all the ingredients on the board in different styles according to your taste.
2. Serve fresh.

Nutrition per Serving:

Calories: 398 | Fat: 26g | Carbohydrates: 43g | Protein: 66g | Sugar: 15g | Fiber: 8g | Potassium: 1021mg | Sodium: 1340mg | Cholesterol: 50mg

4.3 Charcuterie board with all food groups

Preparation time: 15 mins | Cooking time: 0 mins | Servings: 2

Ingredients

- Boiled egg, 1
- Tomato, 1
- Cucumber, Cabbage, bell pepper, spinach (1 cup/250g)
- Egg sandwiches, 4
- Hotdogs, 2
- Rice boiled, ¾ cup (155g)
- Olives, as needed.
- Pieces of bread in different shapes, as needed.
- Tortilla, 1 or 2
- Shredded cottage cheese, ½ cup (150g)
- Berries (your choice), 1 cup (200g)
- Rosemary, as needed.

Procedure

1. Arrange vegetables in one part of the board.
2. Arrange sandwiches, tortillas, cheese, hotdogs, and berries in another part.
3. Place egg, olives, and tomatoes on the side of the board, and garnish the board with rosemary and lemon.

Nutrition per Serving:

Calories: 289 | Fat: 4g | Carbohydrates: 44g | Protein: 7g | Sugar: 3g | Fiber: 4g | Potassium: 213mg | Sodium: 250mg | Cholesterol: 150mg

4.4 Charcuterie board with grapes and bread

Preparation time: 15 mins | Cooking time: 0 mins | Servings: 6

Ingredients

- Olives, 1 cup (200g)
- Almonds, ½ cup (120g)
- Honey, 3 oz (80ml)
- Peppered Salami, 8 oz (480g)
- Asiago cheese, 8 oz (420g)
- Italian dry salami, 7 oz (400g)
- Red grapes, 1 cup (250g)
- Fresh fig, 1
- French bread, 1 loaf.
- Rosemary, as needed.

Procedure

1. Before serving, let the cheese rest so it may reach room temperature for the best flavor.
2. Place honey, almonds, and mixed olives on or near the board in small serving basins or containers.
3. Asiago cheese should be cut into triangles or smaller bits.
4. Slice the peppered salami into rounds that are 14 inches thick.
5. Place the French bread, cheeses, and meats on the board.
6. Fill in the remaining spots on the board with the grapes, figs, and rosemary sprigs before serving.

Nutrition per Serving:

Calories: 390 | Fat: 15g | Carbohydrates: 6g | Protein: 16g | Sugar: 4g | Fiber: 3g | Potassium: 743mg | Sodium: 1240mg | Cholesterol: 40mg

4.5 Charcuterie board for the weekend

Preparation time: 18 mins |
Cooking time: 0 mins | Servings: 8

Ingredients

- Eggs (hard-boiled), 8
- Cooked sausages, 8 links
- Mini toasted waffles, 16 pieces
- Mini toasted pancakes, 8
- Mini muffins,8
- Yogurt, 2 cups (500g)
- Fresh fruits, 1 cup (250g)
- Syrup, a drizzle.
- Jelly, 4 oz (120g)

Procedure

1. Place the yogurt bowl in the center of the board.
2. Surround it with eggs, muffins, waffles, and pancakes.
3. Pour a drizzle of syrup on the pancakes.
4. Fill the remaining board with fresh fruits, sausages, and jelly.

Nutrition per Serving:

Calories: 285 | Fat: 5g | Carbohydrates: 27g | Protein: 9g | Sugar: 18g | Fiber: 3g | Potassium: 243mg | Sodium: 540mg | Cholesterol: 190mg

4.6 Charcuterie board with immunity boosters

Preparation time: 10 mins |
Cooking time: 0 mins | Servings: 6

Ingredients

- Oranges slices, 3.
- Blood oranges slices, 3
- Brie cheese, 6 oz (360g)
- Cubed fetta cheese, 8 oz (480g)
- Beet chips, 2 cups (250g)
- Dark chocolate, as needed.
- Crackers, 1 cup (250g)
- Almonds, 1 cup (200g)
- Chocolate beans, as needed for garnish.

Procedure

1. Fill the center of the board with fruits.
2. Surround it with crackers, chocolate, beet chips, and cheese,
3. Fill the remaining board with almonds and garnish with chocolate-covered beans.

Nutrition per Serving:

Calories: 300 | Fat: 17g | Carbohydrates: 5g | Protein: 24g | Sugar: 24g | Fiber: 4g | Potassium: 339mg | Sodium: 631mg | Cholesterol: 35mg

4.7 Charcuterie board with tacos

Preparation time: 10 mins | Cooking time: 0 mins | **Serving - 6**

Ingredients

- Guacamole, 1 cup (250g)
- Salsa, 1 cup (250g)
- Taco shells, 6 soft and 6 hard
- Queso, 1 cup (250g)
- Grounded turkey, 1 cup (250g)
- Lettuce, 4-5 leaves
- Tomatoes diced, 1 cup (250g)
- Cheddar cheese (shredded), 1 cup (200g)
- Onions chopped, 1 cup (200g)
- Sour cream, 1 cup (250g)

Procedure

1. Fill the center of the board with tacos shells.
2. Surround it with bowls containing guacamole, salsa, queso, ground turkey, diced tomatoes, chopped onions, shredded cheese, and sour cream.
3. Place lettuce on the side. It's ready to make your tacos.

Nutrition per Serving:

Calories: 226 | Fat: 12g | Carbohydrates: 22g | Protein: 12g | Sugar: 3g | Fiber: 4g | Potassium: 164mg | Sodium: 571mg | Cholesterol: 60mg

4.8 Charcuterie board with multiple snacks

Preparation time: 15 mins |
Cooking time: 0 mins | Servings: 5

Ingredients

- Shredded cheddar cheese, 4 oz (240g)
- crackers (Whole wheat), 1 cup (200g)
- Salami, 6 oz (360g)
- Apple sliced, 1 cup (250g)
- Grapefruit, 1
- Baby carrots, 1 cup (250g)
- Sliced strawberries, 1 cup (250g)
- Green grapes, 1 cup (250g)
- Edamame pods steamed, 1 cup (250g)
- Goldfish crackers baked, 1 cup (250g)
- Apricots dried, 1 cup (250g)
- Blueberries dried, 1 cup (250g)
- Pistachios, 1 cup (250g)
- Ranch dip, 1 cup (250g)
- Walnuts, 1 cup (250g)
- Peanut butter, 1 cup (200g)

Procedure

1. Place backed goldfish, pistachios, peanut butter, and ranch dip in bowls at the edges of the board.
2. Arrange the remaining food items in the middle according to your taste.

Nutrition per Serving:

Calories: 321 | Fat: 13g | Carbohydrates: 21g | Protein: 6g | Sugar: 17g | Fiber: 6g | Potassium: 234mg | Sodium: 873mg | Cholesterol: 25mg

4.9 Charcuterie board with hummus

Preparation time: 15 mins |
Cooking time: 0 mins | Servings: 5

Ingredients

- Hummus, 2 cups (500g)
- Pitas (Whole wheat), 1 cup (200g)
- Carrot sticks, 1 cup (240g)
- Pretzel sticks, 1 cup (240g)
- Yellow, red, and orange bell peppers, 1 cup (240g)
- cucumber, 1, cut into sticks.
- Crackers, 1 cup (240g)
- Pecans, ½ cup (120g)

Procedure

1. Place hummus bowls in the center of the board.
2. Arrange the remaining food items in the surroundings according to your taste.

Nutrition per Serving:

Calories: 332 | Fat: 5g | Carbohydrates: 30g | Protein: 8g | Sugar: 7g | Fiber: 6g | Potassium: 98mg | Sodium: 456mg | Cholesterol: 0mg

4.10 Charcuterie board for kids' snack

Preparation time: 30 mins |
Cooking time: 0 mins | Servings: 10

Ingredients

- Fresh mixed fruits, 1 cup (250g)
- Chocolate yogurt fruit dip, ¾ cup (200g)
- Cheese & ham pretzel roll-ups, 10
- Bananas dipped in frozen yogurt, 10.
- Mini peppers stuffed with cheese, 5.
- Crackers, 1 cup (250g)

Procedure

1. Place yogurt and mixed fruit bowls in the center of the board.
2. Place bananas, and roll-ups in the corners of the board pointing outwards.
3. Arrange the remaining food items in the surroundings according to your taste.

Nutrition per Serving:

Calories: 245 | Fat: 2g | Carbohydrates: 12g | Protein: 10g | Sugar: 23g | Fiber: 3g | Potassium: 176mg | Sodium: 387mg | Cholesterol: 10mg

4.11 Charcuterie board with fried foods

Preparation time: 20 mins |
Cooking time: 60 mins | Servings: 5

Ingredients

- Coleslaw, 1 cup (180g)
- Sweet onion caramelized, 1.
- Cheese and arugula bread, 2
- Fried onion rings, 10
- Burger meatball skewers, 6
- Ranch dip, 1 cup (200g)
- Baby tomatoes, 7-8
- Chopped carrots, 2.
- Jalapeno peppers, 2
- Texas toasts, 6-7
- Cheese balls, 1 cup (250g)
- Sweet onion & sausage, 2

Procedure

1. Fry the ingredients which need to be fried.
2. Arrange all the items on the board in a beautiful style of your choice.
3. Place coleslaw and ranch dip in the bowls on the board.
4. Serve fresh.

Nutrition per Serving:

Calories: 411 | Fat: 11g | Carbohydrates: 28g | Protein: 21g | Sugar: 2g | Fiber: 4g | Potassium: 216mg | Sodium: 875mg | Cholesterol: 40mg

4.12 Rainbow Charcuterie board

Preparation time: 20 mins |
Cooking time: 0 mins | Servings: 4

Ingredients

- Pear, 1
- Whole wheat pita, 8
- Yellow, green, and orange bell pepper, 1 cup sliced (250g)
- Cucumber sticks, 4-5
- Baby carrot sticks, 4-5
- Hummus, 2 cups (400g)
- Dried fruit, ½ cup (125g)
- Cheese cubes, 1 cup (250g)
- Pecans, ½ cup (125g)
- Almonds, ½ cup (125g)
- Candy eyes, 2

Procedure

1. Put the pear in the center. Put candy eyes on it.
2. Surround it with cheese pointed outwards and fill the points with dried fruit.
3. Then place vegetable sticks around it like a fan pointing outwards.
4. Place hummus and almonds in separate bowls and place them on the edges.
5. Fill the board with the remaining food items.

Nutrition per Serving:

Calories: 214 | Fat: 5g | Carbohydrates: 11g | Protein: 22g | Sugar: 5g | Fiber: 5g | Potassium: 114mg | Sodium: 285mg | Cholesterol: 15mg

4.13 Watermelon Charcuterie board

Preparation time: 15 mins | Cooking time: 0 mins | Servings: 8

Ingredients

- Watermelon, 1 medium
- Cucumbers, 2
- Green grapes, 1 cup (200g)
- Sliced radishes, 1 cup (200g)
- Raspberries, 1 cup (200g)
- Brie cheese, 1 cup (200g)
- Crackers, 1 cup (200g)
- Almonds and pistachios, 1 cup (200g)
- Pomegranates, 2
- Marshmallows, 1 cup (200g)
- Honey, 2 tbsp (30g)

Procedure

1. Cut watermelon into different shapes.
2. Cut cucumbers with a star cookie cutter.
3. Place them in style on the board and surround them with remaining ingredients.
4. Place honey and marshmallows in separate bowls and place them on the edges.

Nutrition per Serving:

Calories: 253 | Fat: 3.2g | Carbohydrates: 37g | Protein: 4.5g | Sugar: 21g | Fiber: 4.5g | Potassium: 641mg | Sodium: 255mg | Cholesterol: 25mg

4.14 Charcuterie board with deserts

Preparation time: 10 mins | Cooking time: 0 mins| Servings: 5

Ingredients

- Almonds covered with milk chocolate, 1 cup (250g)
- Cookies, 2 Pack
- Green grapes, 1 cup (200g)
- Almond crisps, 1 cup (200g)
- Ganache dip, 2 cup (400g)
- Berries, 1 cup (200g)
- Pretzel sticks dipped in chocolate, 1 cup (200g)
- Chocolate salami, 1 cup (200g)
- Orange peel, ¼ cup (62g)
- Shortbread with filling, 6-7

Procedure

1. Place the chocolate ganache dip in two bowls. Put them someplace close to the middle of your serving board.
2. Around the dips on the board, scatter grapes, berries, sweets, cookies, shortbread, pretzels, orange peel, almonds crisps, and salami. Cover with a lid and store it in the refrigerator.

Nutrition per Serving:

Calories: 512 | Fat: 18g | Carbohydrates: 49g | Protein: 9g | Sugar: 57g | Fiber: 4g | Potassium: 369mg | Sodium: 953mg | Cholesterol: 10mg

4.15 Green Charcuterie board

Preparation time: 10 mins | Cooking time: 0 mins | Servings: 7

Ingredients

- Triple cream cheese, 8 oz (450g)
- Blue cheese, 8 oz (450g)
- Burrata cheese, 8 oz (450g)
- Summer sausage, 3-4
- Olives, 1 cup (250g)
- Green vegetables, 2 cups (450g)
- Pepperonis, 1 cup (200g)
- Dried fruit, 1 cup (200g)
- Mini toasted crackers, 1 cup (200g)

Procedure

1. Arrange all the ingredients on the board in different styles according to your taste.
2. Serve fresh.

Nutrition per Serving:

Calories: 240 | Fat: 16g | Carbohydrates: 15g | Protein: 10g | Sugar: 7g | Fiber: 3g | Potassium: 120mg | Sodium: 607mg | Cholesterol: 35mg

4.16 Spanish Charcuterie board

Preparation time: 60 mins | Cooking time: 60 mins | Servings: 8

Ingredients

- Tomato sauce, 1 cup (200g)
- Potatoes baked, 1 cup (200g)
- cured chorizo, 4 oz (115g)
- Olives, 1 cup (100g)
- Manchego cheese, 9 oz (250g)
- Serrano ham, 4 oz (115g)
- Iberic ham, 4 oz (115g)
- Dates, 1 cup (175g)
- Fig jam, ½ cup (160g)
- Almonds, ½ cup (73g)
- Oregano, for garnish

Procedure

1. Finish preparing the baked potatoes one hour before serving.
2. Put the tomato sauce on a board when you've finished cooking it. Put the potatoes on a serving dish and position them in corners.
3. The chorizo and ham should be placed around the cheese in the center of the board.
4. Around the board, place the olives, dates, and jam in separate little condiment dishes.
5. The almonds should be used to fill up the vacant area. To give the board some texture and color diversity, scatter the oregano sprigs throughout it.

Nutrition per Serving:

Calories: 560 | Fat: 21g | Carbohydrates: 20g | Protein: 33g | Sugar: 18g | Fiber: 4.5g | Potassium: 763mg | Sodium: 1433mg | Cholesterol: 60mg

4.17 Brunch Charcuterie board

Preparation time: 30 mins |
Cooking time: 0 mins | Servings: 8

Ingredients

- Mini waffles, 6
- Mini pancakes, 6
- Fresh donuts, 6
- Eggs hard-boiled, 6.
- Cheddar cheese, 1 cup (170g)
- Bacon, 7-8 pieces
- Salami, 7-8 pieces
- Salmon smoked, 160g.
- Fresh vegetables as per your choice, 1 cup (250g)
- Fresh fruits, 1 cup (250g)
- Mixed nuts, 1 cup (250g)

Procedure

1. Put the pancakes, donuts, and waffles on a large board.
2. Place the cheese and meat all over the waffles.
3. Use nuts, fruits, and vegetables to fill up the gaps.
4. Use little dishes or cups to provide more depth. For a splash of color, garnish with fresh herbs and flowers. Enjoy.

Nutrition per Serving:

Calories: 521 | Fat: 11g | Carbohydrates: 45g | Protein: 25g | Sugar: 16g | Fiber: 5g | Potassium: 942mg | Sodium: 771mg | Cholesterol: 80mg

4.18 Winter Charcuterie board

Preparation time: 15 mins |
Cooking time: 0 mins | Servings: 10

Ingredients

- Brie cheese, 8 oz (240g)
- Gorgonzola cheese, 8 oz (240g)
- Parmesan cheese, sliced 8 oz (240g)
- Aged cheddar cheese 6 oz (180g)
- Monterey Jack cheese, 6 oz (180g)
- Breadsticks, 18 oz (510g)
- Rosemary crackers, 16 oz (450g)
- Baby apples, 10
- Kumquats, 10
- Persimmons, 2
- Clementines, 2
- Pomegranate arils, ½ cup (60g)
- Pistachios, ½ cup (120g)
- Thyme, as needed.

Procedure

1. On a dish or wooden cheese board, arrange the cheeses, crackers, breadsticks, apples, clementines, kumquats, pomegranate, pistachios, and persimmons.
2. If desired, add thyme as a garnish.

Nutrition per Serving:

Calories: 616 | Fat: 32g | Carbohydrates: 27g | Protein: 29g | Sugar: 9g | Fiber: 6.5g | Potassium: 1666mg | Sodium: 1679mg | Cholesterol: 40mg

4.19 Charcuterie board for picnic

Preparation time: 30 mins | Cooking time: 0 mins | Servings: 2

Ingredients

- Asiago cheese, 8 oz (240g)
- Sweet sopressata, 8 oz (240g)
- Prosciutto, 8 oz (240g)
- Olives, 8 oz (240g)
- Sour cherry spread, 8 oz (240g)
- Artichokes grilled, 8 oz (240g)
- Crostini, 8 oz (240g)

Procedure

1. Place the meats and cheeses around the board first.
2. Around the meat and cheese, put the olives and artichokes next.
3. Crostini should be used to fill any gaps.

Nutrition per Serving:

Calories: 616 | Fat: 32g | Carbohydrates: 27g | Protein: 29g | Sugar: 9g | Fiber: 3.5g | Potassium: 1666mg | Sodium: 1679mg | Cholesterol: 75mg

4.20 Autumn Charcuterie board

Preparation time: 15 mins | Cooking time: 15 mins | Servings: 8

Ingredients

- Pomegranate arils, 1-½ cups (360g)
- Vinegar, 2 tbsp (30g)
- Pomegranate molasses, 1-½ tbsp (22g)
- Mustard, 1 tsp (5g)
- Diced shallot, 1.
- Minced garlic clove, 1
- Grounded cinnamon, ¼ -½ tsp (1-3g)
- Salt, ¼ tsp (1g); Pepper, ¼ tsp (1g)
- Olive oil, 1/3 cup (80g)
- Baguette, sliced, 1 large.
- Your favorite cheese, 1 wedge.
- Roasted Pepper Bruschetta, 1 jar (300g)
- Olive Bruschetta, 1 jar (300g)
- Blue Cheese Stuffed Olives, 1 jar (300g)
- Roasted Red Peppers, 1 jar (300g)
- Ricotta cheese, 1 cup (200g)
- Cured Sausage, 1 stick.
- Pepitas, 2/3 cup roasted (180g)
- Fresh fruits

Procedure

1. In a dish, put the pomegranate arils.
2. Whisk the mustard, shallot, garlic, cinnamon, vinegar, molasses, salt, and pepper in a separate bowl.
3. Several teaspoons of the dressing should be added along with the pomegranate seeds.
4. Set the oven's temperature to 350°F. (177°C) On a baking sheet, arrange the baguette slices and sprinkle with a little olive oil. Until toasted and golden brown, bake for 15 minutes.
5. Place the bread around the pomegranate relish in the center of the board. Additionally, you may use Bruschetta, extra cheese, or fresh seasonal fruits (like apples and pears!).
6. Fill the empty spaces with olives, roasted peppers, and pepitas.

Nutrition per Serving:

Calories: 621 | Fat: 28g | Carbohydrates: 15g | Protein: 49g | Sugar: 17g | Fiber: 7g | Potassium: 1104mg | Sodium: 1812mg | Cholesterol: 50mg

4.21 Mediterranean-style Charcuterie board

Preparation time: 20 mins |
Cooking time: 5 mins | Servings: 8

Ingredients

- Hummus, 1 cup (300g)
- Tzatziki, 1 cup (300g)
- Pita bread, 3
- Vegetables fresh, 1 cup (200g)
- Mixed olives, 3/4 cup (200g)
- Cubed feta cheese, ½ cup (120g)
- Tabbouleh, 1 cup (250g)
- Dolma, 8
- Olive oil, 4 tsp (20g)
- Vegetables, grilled or roasted, 1 cup (250g)
- Fresh herbs for garnish

Procedure

1. Apply 2 tbsp of olive oil on both sides of the pita bread. The pita bread should be warmed thoroughly after being heated at 400°F (204°C) or on a grill for 5 minutes.
2. Make eights out of each pita.
3. On a larger board, arrange the pita bread, hummus, tzatziki, grilled and fresh veggies, olives, feta cheese, tabbouleh, and dolma.
4. Over the hummus and tzatziki, add the last 2 tbsp of olive oil.
5. Serve after adding fresh herbs to the plate.

Nutrition per Serving:

Calories: 239 | Fat: 11g | Carbs: 7g | Protein: 5g | Sugar: 1g | Fiber: 5g | Potassium: 75mg | Sodium: 369mg | Cholesterol: 5mg

4.22 French-style Charcuterie board

Preparation time: 10 mins |
Cooking time: 0 mins | Servings: 10

Ingredients

- Salami, 1-½ lb. (700g)
- Cheese cubes, 1 lb. (½ kg)
- Olives, 1 cup (250g)
- Raw vegetables, grilled, 1 cup.
- Fresh fruit, 1 cup.
- Breadsticks, 12 oz
- Nuts, 3/4 cup.
- Fresh herbs, for garnish

Procedure

1. On a wooden cheese board, arrange the cheeses, salami, breadsticks, fresh fruits, and raw vegetables like broccoli.
2. Place olives in a bowl at the side of the board.
3. Fill the empty spaces with nuts.
4. If desired, add fresh herbs as a garnish.

Nutrition per Serving:

Calories: 316 | Fat: 18g | Carbs: 10g | Protein: 17g | Sugar: 7g | Fiber: 4g | Potassium: 149mg | Sodium: 426mg | Cholesterol: 45mg

4.23 Charcuterie board for holidays

Preparation time: 15 mins |
Cooking time: 10 mins | Servings: 4

Ingredients

- Whole Wheat Flatbreads, 2 packs
- Pecans, 2 oz (60g)
- Cinnamon Paprika Spice, 1 tbsp (15g)
- Chili Flakes, 1 tsp (5g)
- Apricot Jam, 3 tbsp (45g)
- Mustard, 2 tsp (10g)
- Le Gruyere Cheese, 6 oz (180g)
- Gouda Cheese, 5 oz (150g)
- Brie Cheese, 8 oz (240g)
- Red Grapes, 4 oz (120g)

Procedure

1. Preheat the oven to 450°F (232°C).. Cut the flatbread into four squares.
2. Mix the flatbread squares with 1 tsp salt and 2 tbsp of olive oil. Place the squares on a baking sheet and toast for 8 to 10 minutes on the top rack, or until golden. Arrange on the board.
3. Prepare the mustard sauce by combining apricot jam and mustard in a small dish. Add paprika and chili flakes. Transfer to a bowl and place on the board.
4. Cut the Gruyere into thin wedges and spread out on one corner of the board or dish. Cut the Gouda into bite-sized pieces and place them on the corner opposite the Gruyere. Add Brie cheese, pecans, and grapes to fill the remaining spaces.

Nutrition per Serving:

Calories – 930| Fat - 71g | Carbs - 56g | Protein - 49g | Sugar – 26g | Fiber – 5.5g | Potassium - 989mg | Sodium – 1826mg | Cholesterol – 90mg

4.24 Charcuterie board for birthday

Preparation time: 20 mins |
Cooking time: 0 mins| Servings: 10

Ingredients

- Crackers, 16 oz (480g)
- Black chocolate, 8 oz (240g)
- Biscuits/cookies, 16 oz (480g)
- Marshmallows, 8 oz (240g)
- Donuts, 16
- Different kind of fresh fruit, cut into slices, 3 cups (750g)
- Tortillas, 10-12
- Sandwiches, 10-12
- Different types of cheese, 16 oz (480g)
- Minced meat cooked with garlic. 16 oz (480g)
- Yogurt dip 4 oz (120g)
- Ranch dip, 4 oz (120g)
- Vegetables raw, 2-3

Procedure

1. Divide the board into 4 sections.
2. Place the fruit slices in one part of the board.
3. Place vegetables in another section.
4. Place sweets in a section.
5. And fast-food snacks in another section.
6. Place yogurt and ranch dips in small bowls all over the board where its empty.

Nutrition per Serving:

Calories – 121| Fat - 26g | Carbs - 84g | Protein - 29g | Sugar – 43g | Fiber – 6.8g | Potassium - 767mg | Sodium – 2156mg | Cholesterol – 75mg

4.25 Hotdog Charcuterie board

Preparation time: 10 mins |
Cooking time: 0 mins | Servings: 10

Ingredients

- Creamy mashed potatoes, 1 cup (300g)
- Beet chips, 8 oz (240g)
- Potato chips, 8 oz (240g)
- Watermelon cubed, 1 cup (200g)
- Berries mix, 1 cup (200g)
- Hotdog and bun, 10
- Caramelized onion dip, ½ cup (120g)
- Ranch dip, ½ cup (120g)

Procedure

1. Put creamy mashed potato in the middle.
2. Place potato and beet chips around the bowl.
3. Cover two sides with hotdogs.
4. And the remaining two with fruit bowls and dips.

Nutrition per Serving:

Calories – 673 | Fat - 12g | Carbs - 46g | Protein - 14g | Sugar – 25g | Fiber – 3.8g | Potassium - 452mg | Sodium – 879mg | Cholesterol – 45mg

4.26 Charcuterie board BBQ

Preparation time: 20 mins |
Cooking time: 10 mins | Servings: 6

Ingredients

- Medium shrimp, 1 lb. (½ kg)
- Sliced Prosciutto, 5 oz (150g)
- Extra Virgin Olive Oil, 2 tbsp (30g)
- Salt, 1 tsp (5g)
- Deveined large shrimp, 1 lb. (½ kg)
- Garlic Pepper, 2 tbsp (30g)
- Skirt steak, 1 lb. (½ kg)
- Hot Pepper Garlic Sauce, 12 oz (360g)
- Freshly ground black pepper

Procedure

1. Turn the grill's heat up high.
2. Slice some prosciutto into tiny pieces, then wrap them around the shrimp.
3. Using a wooden skewer, thread the shrimp onto it.
4. Once complete, spray the skewers with olive oil and season with salt and pepper.
5. Grill for about 3 minutes on each side over high heat before putting on the board.
6. To coat the large shrimp, put them in a dish with the olive oil, spice, and toss to mix.
7. Put shrimp on skewers and cook for about 4 minutes on each side over high heat.
8. Serve on the board.
9. The skirt steak should be cut into tiny pieces and placed in a basin.
10. Mix thoroughly after adding approximately 1-½ cups of the hot pepper garlic. Cover for at least 4 hours to marinate.
11. Turn on the grill heat. Thread the steak chunks onto the skewers once the grill is ready.
12. Cook for about 4 minutes on each side on a grill set to high heat. Serve on the board.

Nutrition per Serving:

Calories – 673 | Fat - 19g | Carbs - 1g | Protein - 53g | Sugar – 1g | Fiber – 0.3g | Potassium - 1266mg | Sodium – 2465mg | Cholesterol – 125mg

4.27 Charcuterie board Tapas

Preparation time: 5 mins |
Cooking time: 0 mins | Servings: 4

Ingredients

- Spanish meat (any), 1 lb. (½ kg)
- Spanish cheeses (any), 8 oz (240g)
- Olives, 1 cup (200g)
- Bread, 1 loaf.
- Ranch dip, ½ cup (130g)
- Grilled/roasted vegetables, 1 cup (250g)
- Nuts mixed, 1 cup (250g)
- Fruits, 3-4
- Tortillas, 6-10

Procedure

1. Arrange all the ingredients on a serving board or small bowls.
2. Serve fresh.

Nutrition per Serving:

Calories – 673 | Fat - 19g | Carbs - 32g | Protein - 53g | Sugar – 5g | Fiber – 6g | Potassium - 1266mg | Sodium – 2465mg | Cholesterol – 85mg

4.28 Seafood Charcuterie board

Preparation time: 15 mins |
Cooking time: 15 mins | Servings: 2

Ingredients

- Mixed cheeses, ½ lb. (250g)
- Mixed seafood (Crabs, lobsters, clam, shrimps), ½ lb. (250g)
- Fresh fruits, mixed, 1 cup (250g)
- Hard boiled eggs, 4
- Sweet corn, 1 cup (250g)

Procedure

1. Slice the cheeses thinly, then put them on the board.
2. Over a high heat, cook mixed shellfish just until they open.
3. Fruit should be washed and cut into bite-sized pieces.
4. Set everything up on your board and have fun!

Nutrition per Serving:

Calories – 575 | Fat - 25g | Carbs - 32g | Protein - 50g | Sugar – 8g | Fiber – 4g | Potassium - 650mg | Sodium – 1568mg | Cholesterol – 150mg

4.29 Charcuterie board full of grilled veggies

Preparation time: 5 mins |
Cooking time: 30 mins | Servings: 6

Ingredients

- Vinegar, 1/3 cup (80ml)
- Olive oil, 3 tbsp. (45g)
- Basil leaves, 1 tbsp. (15g)
- Minced garlic cloves, 2
- Salt, ¼ tsp. (1.5g)
- Grounded black pepper, 1/8 tsp. (0.5g)
- Sweet peppers, 4
- Fennel ,1 bulb
- Mushrooms, 6 large
- Japanese eggplants, 2
- Zucchini, 2
- Fresh asparagus, 8 oz. (227g)

Procedure

1. Marinate all the vegetables with olive oil, salt, black pepper, basil leaves and garlic.
2. Grilled them for 30 minutes on slow heat.
3. Arrange the vegetables on the board in separate bowls.

Nutrition per Serving:

Calories – 160 | Fat - 3g | Carbs - 30g | Protein - 9g | Sugar – 2g | Fiber – 8g | Potassium - 808mg | Sodium – 742mg | Cholesterol – 0mg

4.30 Charcuterie board with shallot bread

Preparation time: 35 mins |
Cooking time: 40 mins | Servings: 12

Ingredients

- White bread flour, 2 cup (500g)
- Yeast, 1 tsp (7g); Butter, 1-½ tbsp (25g)
- Olive oil, 1 tbsp (17g);
- Shallots, 1 cup (250g)
- Dried figs, ½ cup (125g); Basil leaves
- Whole camembert, 2 cups (2 x 250g)
- Clear honey, 1 tbsp (17g)
- Pine nuts, 1 tbsp (17g); Thyme sprigs, 3

Procedure

1. Mix flour, yeast, sugar, and salt in a bowl. Add 350ml warm water to form a sticky dough; knead and let rise until doubled. Sauté shallots in butter and oil until caramelized.
2. Roll dough into a 25x35 cm rectangle, top with shallots, figs, and basil, leaving a border; roll up and slice into 12. Place on a baking sheet, cover, let rise.
3. Bake in a preheated oven at 200°C for 20 minutes. For cheese, bake in trays for 15 minutes, then top with honey, pine nuts, and thyme.

Nutrition per Serving:

Calories – 500 | Fat - 22g | Carbs - 60g | Protein - 22g | Sugar – 11g | Fiber – 4g | Potassium - 657mg | Sodium – 1400mg | Cholesterol – 25mg

4.31 Charcuterie board for sweet tooth

Preparation time: 20 mins |
Cooking time: 10 mins | Servings: 6

Ingredients

For the chocolate-dipped fruit

- Dark chocolate, 1/3 cup (100g)
- Maple nuts, 3 tbsp (50g)
- Tangerine, 1
- Strawberries, 9
- Dates, 6

For the berry compote

- Blackberries, ½ cup (150g)
- Blueberries, ½ cup (150g)
- Sugar, ¼ cup (75g)

To serve

- Meringue nests, 8
- Gingerbread, 1 cup (250g)
- Popcorn, 2 cups (200g)

Procedure

1. Melt 100g of dark chocolate in a bowl to prepare the chocolate-dipped fruits. 50g maple nuts should be finely ground. Tangerine from segment one is dipped in chocolate, followed by crushed almonds. Repeat with 6 dates and 9 strawberries. To set, transfer to a baking sheet.
2. Start working on your berry compote while the fruit is setting.
3. 75g sugar and 150g each of blueberries and blackberries should be gently heated in a small pan to dissolve the sugar. 3–4 minutes of simmering followed by cooling.
4. To serve, spread the berry compote out on a serving board and encircle it with the chocolate-covered fruit, meringue nests, additional maple nuts, gingerbread, and popcorn.

Nutrition per Serving:

Calories – 256 | Fat - 9g | Carbs - 42g | Protein - 3g | Sugar – 40g | Fiber – 4g | Potassium - 58mg | Sodium – 100mg | Cholesterol – 3mg

4.32 Salmon Charcuterie board

Preparation time: 20 mins |
Cooking time: 45 mins | Servings: 8

Ingredients

- Purple beetroot, 2 cups (600g)
- Fennel bulb, 1 large
- Garlic cloves, 2
- Olive oil, 2 tbsp (30g)
- Apples, 2
- Smoked salmon flakes, 2 cups (2 x 100g packs)
- Watercress, ¼ cup (85g)
- Crème fraiche, 1 tbsp (15g)
- Horseradish sauce, 1 tbsp (15g)

Procedure

1. Melt 100g of dark chocolate in a bowl to prepare the chocolate-dipped fruits. 50g maple nuts should be finely ground. Tangerine from segment one is dipped in chocolate, followed by crushed almonds. Repeat with 6 dates and 9 strawberries.
2. To set, transfer to a baking sheet.
3. Start working on your berry compote while the fruit is setting.
4. 75g sugar and 150g each of blueberries and blackberries should be gently heated in a small pan to dissolve the sugar. 3–4 minutes of simmering followed by cooling.
5. To serve, spread the berry compote out on a serving board and surround it with the chocolate-covered fruit, meringue nests, additional maple nuts, gingerbread, and popcorn.

Nutrition per Serving:

Calories – 136 | Fat - 6g | Carbs - 12g | Protein - 8g | Sugar – 10g | Fiber – 3g | Potassium - 454mg | Sodium – 600mg | Cholesterol – 22mg

4.33 Lunch Charcuterie board

Preparation time: 15 mins |
Cooking time: 15 mins | Servings: 10

Ingredients

- Crusty baguette, 1-½ cup (340g)
- Feta marinated in oil, 1 cup (200g)
- Basil, 1 bunch.
- Olives, 1-1/3 cups (300g)
- Capers ¼ cup (60g)
- Tomatoes, 3
- Red onion, 1/2
- Vinegar, 1 tbs
- Basil pesto, 1/2 cup (120g)
- Prosciutto, 1/3 cup (100g)
- Salami, 3 tbsp (50g)
- Cheddar, 1 cup (200g)
- Grapes, 2 cups (400g)

Procedure

1. Preheat the oven to 220°C (428°F) for standard ovens, or 200°C (392°F) for fan ovens.
2. Spread 2 tbsp of the oil from the marinated feta over the bread before placing it on a baking tray.
3. Bake for about 12 minutes, or until it becomes golden and crisp, after scattering with basil stems.
4. To make a paste, combine the remaining oil from the marinated feta, one-third of the basil leaves, olives, capers, and pickling liquid in a food processor. Season with pepper.
5. Finely chop the other half of the basil leaves. In a small bowl, combine the chopped tomato, onion, vinegar, and chopped basil. Season to taste.
6. On a large board, arrange the bread, grapes, cheeses, prosciutto, pesto, olive paste, and tomato mix. Sprinkle with the remaining basil leaves. Serve.

Nutrition per Serving:

Calories – 554 | Fat - 21g | Carbs - 15g | Protein - 12g | Sugar – 8g | Fiber – 3g | Potassium - 650mg | Sodium – 1438mg | Cholesterol – 25mg

4.34 Caesar Charcuterie board

Preparation time: 20 mins |
Cooking time: 25 mins | Servings: 12

Ingredients

- Bacon, ½ cup (100g)
- Garlic bread, 1-½ cup (330g)
- Peas, ½ cup (100g)
- Garlic aioli, 1 cup (250g)
- Hard-boiled eggs, 4
- Baby cos lettuce, 1
- Celery, 1/2 bunch.
- Cucumber, 1
- Anchovies, 3 tbsp (45g)
- Parmesan, 3 tbsp (40g)

Procedure

1. Lay down the bacon on a tray in a single layer. Place the bread on a different baking sheet, then bake for 15 minutes, or until it become golden and crisp. trays from the oven. To get the bacon brown and crisp, bake it for an additional 10 minutes.
2. In the meantime, put snow peas in a heat-resistant dish. Add boiling water on top. Drain after standing for 4 minutes or until tender.
3. On a big dish, put a small bowl of aioli. On a large board, arrange the bacon, bread, anchovies, lettuce, snow peas, celery, egg, and cucumber,. Add some pepper and parmesan to the dish. Serve.

Nutrition per Serving:

Calories – 333 | Fat - 8g | Carbs - 15g | Protein - 6g | Sugar – 4g | Fiber – 2.5g | Potassium - 227mg | Sodium – 230mg | Cholesterol – 65mg

4.35 Prawn Charcuterie board

Preparation time: 15 mins |
Cooking time: 0 mins | Servings: 8

Ingredients

- Seafood salad, 2 cups (500g)
- Seafood sauce, 1 cup (250g)
- Prawns, 3 cups (700g)
- Oysters, 12
- Parsley, 1 bunch.
- Lettuce, (to garnish)
- Prawn cocktail, 2cups (516g)
- Lemon, 1 (to garnish)

Procedure

1. Put a bowl in the middle of the board and fill it with the seafood sauce.
2. The oysters should be placed on top of lettuce.
3. On the board, arrange the cocktail prawns with tails.
4. Onto the board, arrange the prawns.
5. Spread out the seafood salad mix on the board.
6. Lemons should be sliced into eighths and placed around the board as a garnish. Put the parsley in the middle, in between the prawns.

Nutrition per Serving:

Calories – 787 | Fat - 23g | Carbs - 12g | Protein - 46g | Sugar – 10g | Fiber – 1g | Potassium - 1432mg | Sodium – 1886mg | Cholesterol – 212mg

4.36 Charcuterie board with meat and pickles

Preparation time: 10 mins |
Cooking time: 10 mins | Servings: 6

Ingredients

- Sourdough, 1 medium loaf
- Olive oil, 2 tbsp (33g)
- Basil pesto, 1/3 cup (100g)
- Capsicum pesto, 1/3 cup (100g)
- Chorizo, 1/3 cup (100g)
- Parma ham, 2 oz (40g)
- Hummus, 1/3 cup (100g)
- Pickles, ¼ cup (50g)
- Wesendale, ¼ cup (50g)
- Brie cheese, ¼ cup (50g)
- Cheddar cheese, ¼ cup (50g)

Procedure

1. Preheat the oven to 180°C (356°F). Slice the sourdough and place on a baking sheet. Drizzle with olive oil and toast in the oven for 5 minutes.
2. Slice the cheeses and allow them to come to room temperature. Then, arrange all the ingredients on a serving platter.

Nutrition per Serving:

Calories – 720 | Fat - 28g | Carbs - 8g | Protein - 52g | Sugar – 13g | Fiber – 2g | Potassium - 932mg | Sodium – 1706mg | Cholesterol – 65mg

4.37 Charcuterie board for big party

Preparation time: 20 mins |
Cooking time: 0 mins | Servings: 25

Ingredients

- Jatz, 2 boxes
- Salami, 1/3 cup (100g)
- Prosciutto, 1/3 cup (100g)
- Brie cheese, 8 oz (240g)
- Cheddar cheese, 8 oz (240g)
- Blue cheese, 8 oz (240g)
- Camembert, ½ cup (125g)
- Hummus, 4 cups (1kg)
- Olive oil, 1 tsp (5ml)
- Zaatar, 1 tsp (5g)
- Grapes, 1 bunch.
- Apricots, 1 cup (250g)
- Punnet fig, 1
- Nuts, 1/3 cup (100g)
- Olives, 1 cup (250g)
- Baby cucumber, 1

Procedure

1. Create your own snacking board by arranging the items on your favorite cheeseboard or serving tray using instruction from the introduction.

Nutrition per Serving:

Calories – 522 | Fat - 19g | Carbs - 12g | Protein - 43g | Sugar – 23g | Fiber – 2.5g | Potassium - 1066mg | Sodium – 2004mg | Cholesterol – 72mg

4.38 Egg day Charcuterie board

Preparation time: 10 mins |
Cooking time: 10 mins | Servings: 6

Ingredients

- Olive Oil, 1 tsp (5ml)
- Eggs, 6
- Quinoa Bread Loaf, ½
- Red Onion, ½
- Vinegar, 1 tbsp (15ml)
- Dill, ½ bunch
- Cream Cheese, 1 cup (225g)
- Capers, 1 tbsp (9g)
- Lemon, 1 (½ cut into wedges, juice of other ½)
- Smoked Salmon, 1 cup (150g)
- Avocado, 1

Procedure

1. Preheat the oven to 200°C (392°F). Spray 6 muffin tins with olive oil sparingly. Crack an egg into each hole. Lightly oil both sides of the bread and place on a baking sheet.
2. Toast the bread in the oven alongside the eggs. The bread should be toasted, the egg whites set, and the yolk cooked to your preference after about 15 minutes.
3. In the meanwhile, place the red onion and vinegar in a small dish, cover, and refrigerate until needed. Finely chop the dill, then mix with cream cheese, capers, and the juice of ½ the lemon in a bowl. Season with black pepper.
4. On a large board, arrange the following: smoked salmon, baked eggs, sliced avocado, toast, drained pickled onion, lemon wedges, and the cream cheese mixture. Sprinkle with remaining chopped dill and season with black pepper to taste.

Nutrition per Serving:

Calories – 369 | Fat - 8g | Carbs - 12g | Protein - 16g | Sugar – 3g | Fiber – 4g | Potassium - 452mg | Sodium – 431mg | Cholesterol – 187mg

4.39 Sweet potato charcuterie board

Preparation time: 10 mins |
Cooking time: 30 mins | Servings: 4

Ingredients

- Tomatoes, 1- ½ cup (320g)
- Red capsicum, 1
- Large carrot, 1
- Red onion, 1 small
- Sweet potatoes, 4
- Olive oil, 2 tbsp (30 ml)
- Hummus, 1 cup (240g)
- Kale leaves, 3
- Beetroot hummus, 1 cup (240g)
- Guacamole, 1 cup (230g)

Procedure

1. Preheat the oven to 220°C (428°F). Place the sweet potatoes in a mixing bowl, add 1 tbsp of the olive oil, and toss to coat. Bake in the oven for 40 minutes, or until soft.
2. In the meantime, add the remaining olive oil to the kale leaves torn into 6 cm pieces in the same bowl, and then massage with oil until softened. Place the kale on a separate tray in an even layer. On the same tray, arrange the tomatoes and the red capsicum. Place both pans in the oven, and bake for 15 minutes, or until the vegetables are tender and the kale is crisp. Arrange the kale, tomatoes, and capsicum on a large serving board.
3. Remove the potatoes from the oven. Make a slit in each, then slightly open them up. Arrange the potatoes, carrot, and red onion on the serving board.
4. Place the hummus, beetroot hummus, and guacamole in small bowls and place them in the center of the board.

Nutrition per Serving:

Calories – 618 | Fat - 27g | Carbs - 54g | Protein - 15g | Sugar – 33g | Fiber – 11g | Potassium - 434mg | Sodium – 851mg | Cholesterol – 0mg

4.40 Ice cream charcuterie board

Preparation time: 15 mins |
Cooking time: 0 mins | Servings: 8

Ingredients

- Waffles, 4
- Chocolate sauce, ½ cup (120g)
- Honeycomb, 6 pieces
- Oreos, 6
- Roasted peanuts, ½ cup (120g)
- Colored sprinkles, ¼ cup (60g)
- Strawberries, 1 cup (250g)
- Vanilla ice-cream, 1L

Procedure

1. In separate dishes or on a board or tray, arrange all the ingredients aside from the ice cream.
2. Fill 8 cups or jars with ice cream.

Nutrition per Serving:

Calories – 716 | Fat - 15g | Carbs - 22g | Protein - 5g | Sugar – 78g | Fiber – 2g | Potassium - 120mg | Sodium – 1342mg | Cholesterol – 30mg

5 DRINKS FOR CHARCUTERIE

5.1 Ginger-pear mocktail

Preparation time: 5 mins |
Cooking time: 0 mins | Servings: 8

Ingredients

- Sliced pear, 4.
- Simple pear syrup, 16 tsp (80ml)
- Ginger beer, 8 cup (2L)
- Vodka (pear-flavored), 32 oz (1L)
- Lime juice, 1 squeezed.
- Mint leaves

Procedure

1. Mix the pear slices and pear simple syrup in a cocktail shaker.
2. Combine fresh mint with one lime wedge after it has been squeezed.
3. Make a shake using vodka and ginger beer.
4. Add a slice of pears as a garnish and pour the mixture into a cocktail glass with ice.

Nutrition per Serving:

Calories – 127 | Fat - 0g | Carbs - 16g | Protein - 0g | Sugar – 1g | Fiber – 1g | Potassium - 87mg | Sodium – 1mg | Cholesterol – 0mg

5.2 Mint peach julep

Preparation time: 5 mins |
Cooking time: 0 mins | Servings: 6

Ingredients

- White peach, 3
- Sugar, 6 tsp (30g)
- Bourbon whisky, 15 oz (500ml)
- Peach liquor, 15 oz (500ml)
- Mint leaves, 42 springs

Procedure

1. Add the peach dice, sugar, and mint sprigs to a cocktail shaker. till fragrant, stir.
2. Add the peach liqueur and bourbon. Shake thoroughly after adding ice to the shaker.
3. Put some mint on top after straining into glasses.

Nutrition per Serving:

Calories – 111 | Fat - 0g | Carbs - 14g | Protein - 0.2g | Sugar – 1g | Fiber – 1g | Potassium - 7mg | Sodium – 0.9mg | Cholesterol – 0mg

5.3 Champagne drink

Preparation time: 5 mins |
Cooking time: 0 mins | Servings: 4

Ingredients

- Champagne
- Sugar, 4 tsp (20g)
- Dashes of bitter, 8
- Brandy, 8 tsp (40ml)

Procedure

1. Fill the bottom of each Champagne flute with a sugar cube.
2. Each flute should contain two dashes of bitters, which you should allow sit for 30 seconds.
3. Pour 2 tablespoons of brandy into each flute.
4. Champagne should be poured completely into each glass.

Nutrition per Serving:

Calories – 128 | Fat - 0g | Carbs - 8g | Protein - 0.2g | Sugar – 8g | Fiber – 0g | Potassium - 7mg | Sodium – 2mg | Cholesterol – 0mg

5.4 Iced coffee for cookies board.

Preparation time: 10 mins |
Cooking time: 0 mins | Servings: 2

Ingredients

- Chocolate mix, 2 tbsp (30g)
- Instant coffee, 2 tbsp (30g)
- Splenda, 6 packs
- Hot water, 4 oz (100ml)
- Coldwater, 10 oz (280ml)
- Milk, 4 oz
- Coffee creamer, 2 tbsp(30g)
- Ice

Procedure

1. In a 16 oz. glass, combine the breakfast mix, coffee, Splenda, and hot water.
2. Add milk, coffee creamer, and iced water. Stir.
3. Ice should fill the cup all the way up.

Nutrition per Serving:

Calories – 80 | Fat - 0.1g | Carbs - 15g | Protein - 3g | Sugar – 8g | Fiber – 0.5g | Potassium - 135mg | Sodium – 58mg | Cholesterol – 2mg

5.5 Lime drink

Preparation time: 10 mins | Cooking time: 0 mins | Servings: 4

Ingredients

- Water, 4 cups (1L)
- Sugar, 1 cup (250g)
- Salt, 1 tsp (5g)
- Lemon juice, 4 tbsp (60ml)
- Lime juice, 4 tbsp (60ml)
- Cold water
- Ice

Procedure

1. Combine boiling water, sugar, and salt until completely dissolved.
2. Pour in the juice.
3. Fill a one-quart container halfway with ice. Chill by stirring.
4. Fill the rest of the container with water and mix thoroughly.
5. Serve.

Nutrition per Serving:

Calories – 208 | Fat - 0.1g | Carbs - 55g | Protein - 0.2g | Sugar – 51g | Fiber – 0.1g | Potassium - 74mg | Sodium – 582mg | Cholesterol – 0mg

5.6 Beer margarita

Preparation time: 10 mins | Cooking time: 0 mins | Servings: 2

Ingredients

- Limeade, 6 oz (150ml)
- Light beer, 6 oz (150ml)
- Tequilla,4 oz (120ml)
- Powdered sugar, 1 tsp (5g)
- Ice

Procedure

1. Mix in blender.
2. Serve.

Nutrition per Serving:

Calories – 190 | Fat - 0g | Carbs - 12g | Protein - 0.2g | Sugar – 10g | Fiber – 0g | Potassium - 28mg | Sodium – 5mg | Cholesterol – 0mg

5.7 Peach and white wine punch

Preparation time: 30 mins | Cooking time: 0 mins | Servings: 7

Ingredients

- White wine
- Peach flavor vodka
- Diet sprite
- Frozen peaches
- Frozen mangoes
- Frozen raspberries
- Sliced apple.

Procedure

1. Combine white wine, peach vodka, and half of the diet sprite.
2. Fruit should be sliced and/or thawed.
3. Slowly add the fruit into the wine/vodka/Sprite mixture.
4. Place it in the refrigerator to cool overnight.
5. Remove when ready to serve.
6. To make it bubbly, add the rest of the diet sprite.

Nutrition per Serving:

Calories – 190 | Fat - 0.2g | Carbs - 11g | Protein - 0.6g | Sugar – 6g | Fiber – 1g | Potassium - 188mg | Sodium – 17mg | Cholesterol – 0mg

5.8 Pomegranate mocktail

Preparation time: 5 mins | Cooking time: 0 mins | Servings: 2

Ingredients

- 100% pomegranate juice, 6 oz (180ml)
- Diet tonic water, 6 oz (180ml)

Procedure

1. Fill Cocktail glass with ice.
2. Tonic Water with Pomegranate juice

Nutrition per Serving:

Calories – 190 | Fat - 0g | Carbs - 14g | Protein - 0.4g | Sugar – 12g | Fiber – 0.5g | Potassium - 225mg | Sodium – 13mg | Cholesterol – 0mg

5.9 Cream-whiskey cocktail

Preparation time: 5 mins |
Cooking time: 0 mins | Servings: 2

Ingredients

- Whiskey, 2 FL oz (60ml)
- Milk, 2 cups (400ml)
- Instant coffee mix, 2 FL oz (60ml)
- Sweetener, 2
- Ice

Procedure

1. Mix all the ingredients well.
2. Serve.

Nutrition per Serving:

Calories – 150 | Fat - 0g | Carbs - 18g | Protein - 8.4g | Sugar – 0g | Fiber – 0g | Potassium - 415mg | Sodium – 128mg | Cholesterol – 8mg

5.10 Watermelon mojito

Preparation time: 120 mins |
Cooking time: 0 mins | Servings: 4

Ingredients

- Watermelon frozen cubes, 3 cups
- Lime, 5
- Rum, 6 oz (180ml)
- Splenda, 2 tbsp (30g)
- Fresh mint

Procedure

1. Cut the watermelon into tiny pieces.
2. Put in a sturdy zip-locked freezer bag and freeze until ready to use.
3. Squeeze 4 limes to yield 6 tablespoons of juice.
4. Blend frozen cubes in a blender. Blend until smooth.
5. Combine fresh mint leaves and fresh lime juice in a small pitcher.
6. Smash the lime and mint leaves several times with a wooden spoon to release the mint oils.
7. Pour rum and the pureed frozen watermelon into the pitcher and mix carefully.
8. Sweeten with Splenda to taste.
9. Garnish with a wedge of watermelon, lime slices, and/or mint sprigs.

Nutrition per Serving:

Calories – 205 | Fat - 0g | Carbs - 54g | Protein - 0g | Sugar – 0g | Fiber – 1g | Potassium - 37mg | Sodium – 1mg | Cholesterol – 0mg

6 VEGETARIAN CHARCUTERIE BOARDS

6.1 Cheesy Vegetarian Charcuterie Board

Preparation Time: 25 min | Cooking time: 0 min | Servings: 4

Ingredients

- Hummus and guacamole spreads, 8oz each (240g each)
- Cheddar and blue cheese, 5oz each (150g each)
- Carrots, 2
- Celery stalk, 1
- Olives, ½ cup (125g)
- Sundried tomatoes, 1 cup (250g)
- Grilled Artichokes, 1 cup (250g)
- Blackberries, a handful
- Red/green grapes, a handful
- Figs, a handful
- Mixed nuts,1/2 cup (125g)
- Pita bread, 1

Procedure

1. Start making homemade spreads (such as hummus and guacamole) first.
2. Start putting the board together once you've gathered all of the other supplies. Spreads, small bowls, and cheese should be put on the board first before the smaller items (see step-by-step photos or video).
3. All the remaining smaller components should be added after that.
4. Add a tiny bit more of each item to fill in the gaps (or the ones you like best).
5. Serve immediately and enjoy with some bread on the side!

Nutrition per Serving:

Calories – 1055kcal | Fat - 79g | Carbs - 60g | Protein - 41g | Sugar – 11g | Fiber – 8g | Potassium - 1739mg | Sodium – 2136mg | Cholesterol – 50mg

6.2 Summer Fruit and Cheese Board

Preparation Time: 45 min | Cooking time: 0 min | Servings: 16

Ingredients

- Green and black olives, 1 cup (250g)
- Olive oil, 2 tbsp (30g)
- Fresh parsley, 4tbsp (60g)
- Basil, 1 tbsp (15g)
- Chives, 2 tbsp (30g)
- Goat cheese, 8oz (240g)
- Whole grain baguette, 48 slices
- Peaches/plums, 1 and ½ cups (375g)
- Berries, 1 and ½ cups (375)
- Zucchini, 1cup (250g)
- Carrots, 1cup (250g)
- Cherry tomatoes, 1cup (250g)
- Hard-aged cheese and soft-ripened cheese, 8oz each
- Mixed nuts, 1 cup (250g)
- Red pepper, a pinch

Procedure

1. Mix olives with basil, red pepper, and oil; transfer to a serving dish. Coat goat cheese with chives on a plate. Grill oiled baguette slices to a crisp.
2. Assemble a cheese board starting with cherry tomatoes, berries, peaches, zucchini, and carrots at the center.
3. Arrange cheeses, followed by grilled bread, crackers, and sausage.
4. Place the olive dish on the board and sprinkle nuts in empty spaces.
5. Optionally, decorate with edible flowers and mint.

Nutrition facts/values(per serving)

Calories – 460kcal | Fat - 32g | Carbs - 27g | Protein - 25g | Sugar – 3g | Fiber – 5g | Potassium - 259mg | Sodium – 900mg | Cholesterol – 30mg

6.3 Fiesta Avocado Appetizer Board

Preparation time: 15 min | Cooking time: 0 min | Servings: 15

Ingredient/Food list

- Avocado black bean dip, 2cups (500g)
- Bell peppers, 2 cups (500g)
- Baked tortilla chips, 4 cups(1000g)
- Lime, 1
- Colby Jack cheese, 6oz (180g)
- Roasted red peppers, 6oz (180g)
- Cherry tomatoes, 1 and ½ cups (375g)
- Mango, 1
- Cilantro, ¼ cup (62.5g)

Procedure

1. Put the guacamole or dip in a medium serving bowl. If desired, add lime wedges as a garnish. Put the bowl close to the board's center.
2. Arrange tortilla chips and bell pepper halves on either end of the board, covering all four corners.
3. Place the chips, pepper halves, and cheese slices on the board in three distinct portions. Slices of roasted red pepper should be placed on one of the board's open corners in a small bowl.
4. Place mango chunks on either side of the dipping basin. Add cilantro sprigs on the board as decoration.

Nutrition per Serving:

Calories – 185kcal | Fat - 9g | Carbs - 18g | Protein - 7g | Sugar – 6g | Fiber – 4g | Potassium - 405.1mg | Sodium – 257mg | Cholesterol – 10mg

6.4 Nordic-pickled Appetizer Board

Preparation Time: 40 min | Cooking time: 1 day | Servings: 16

Ingredients

Refrigerated Pickles

- Mixed vegetables, 2 cups (500g)
- White vinegar, 2 and ½ cups (625g)
- Water, 1 and ½ cups (375g)
- Sugar, 4 tsp (20g)
- Kosher salt, 1 and ½ tsp (7.5g)
- Fresh dill, 3-4 sprigs
- Coriander seeds, ¾ tsp (3.75g)
- Mustard seeds, ¾ tsp (3.75g)
- Black peppercorns, ¾ tsp (3.75g)

Appetizer Board

- Plain skier, ½ cup
- Refrigerator pickles, 1 recipe
- Rye toasts, 8
- Half cucumber
- Medium tomatoes, 2
- Boiled eggs, 3
- Capers, 3 tbsp (45g)
- Lemon wedges, salt, and black pepper to taste.

Procedure

1. Slice the vegetables, then pack them tightly into the jars to make pickles. Mix the dill (or fennel fronds), coriander, mustard seeds, peppercorns, sugar, water, vinegar, salt, and mustard seeds in a medium pot. Bring to a simmer for about 4 minutes over medium-high heat. Pour the brine over the vegetables. For it to get to room temperature, allow one hour. Place for at least 24 hours in the refrigerator before serving.
2. Set a bowl of skyr on a big plate or board. Put the pickles, rye toast (or crackers), capers, cucumber, tomatoes, salmon, lemon wedges, and eggs on the dish.

Nutrition facts/values (per serving)

Calories – 73kcal | Fat - 4g | Carbs - 8g | Protein - 2g | Sugar – 3g | Fiber – 1.5g | Potassium - 133mg | Sodium – 275mg | Cholesterol – 35mg

6.5 Unique Salad Appetizer Board

Preparation Time: 45 min |
Cooking time: 45 min | Servings: 6

Ingredients

- Creamy Herb Dressing
- Buttermilk, ½ cup (125g)
- Mayonnaise, 2 tbsp (30g)
- Plain Yogurt, 2tsp (10g)
- Honey, black pepper, and kosher salt, ½ tsp each (2.5g)
- Scallion and garlic clove 1 each
- Lemon juice

Marinated Peaches

- Medium peaches, 2
- White vinegar, 2tbsp (30g)
- Fresh parsley, 1 tbsp (15g)
- Small shallot, half
- Kosher salt, ¼ tsp (1.25g)

Salad Board

- Mixed salad greens, 12 cups(3000g)
- Corn kernels, 2 ears
- Cherry tomatoes, 1 cup (250g)
- Hard-boiled eggs, 4
- String beans, 8oz
- Half cucumber
- Goat cheese, 6oz
- Large avocado, 1

Procedure

1. Whisk together buttermilk, yogurt, mayonnaise, lemon juice, salt, pepper, garlic, scallion, honey, and mustard to make the dressing; set in a small jar.
2. Toss peaches with vinegar, shallot, salt, and parsley; let marinate. Combine greens, corn, and eggs; lay out on a salad board with a bowl for greens and another for marinated peaches.
3. Arrange cucumbers, tomatoes, radishes, string beans, avocado, and goat cheese around these bowls. Place the dressing jar and serve immediately.

Nutrition per Serving:

Calories – 410kcal | Fat - 24g | Carbs - 28g | Protein - 18g | Sugar – 10g | Fiber – 7g | Potassium - 1080mg | Sodium – 615mg | Cholesterol – 150mg

6.6 Ultimate Cheese plate with Roasted Grapes

Preparation Time: 15 min |
Cooking time: 15 min | Servings: 6

Ingredients

- Purple and green grapes, 1cup
- Extra virgin olive oil, 2tbsp (30g)
- Thyme and rosemary, 4 sprigs each
- Kosher salt and black pepper to taste.
- Ricotta, brie, and cheddar cheese, 6oz each
- Figs, 8
- Smoked almonds, 1 cup.
- Crackers and sliced baguette

Procedure

1. Place parchment paper on a baking pan and preheat the oven to 450°F (232°C).
2. Arrange the grapes on the baking sheet in bunches. Toss the grapes in a bowl with olive oil, salt, and pepper. Place the grapes amid the thyme and rosemary.
3. Roast the grapes for 12 to 15 minutes. Place the grapes in the middle of a sizable board. Surround the grapes with ricotta, Brie, cheddar, almonds, and figs. Serve with a baguette and crackers.

Nutrition per Serving:

Calories – 538kcal | Fat - 35g | Carbs - 30g | Protein - 19g | Sugar – 22g | Fiber – 3g | Potassium - 874mg | Sodium – 589mg | Cholesterol – 90mg

6.7 Vegan Charcuterie Board with smoky beans on Toast

Preparation Time: 5 min |
Cooking time: 10 min | Servings: 10

Ingredients

- Baguette/Toasted Bread, 10 slices
- Drained cannellini beans, 15oz (420g)
- Extra virgin olive oil, 2tbsp (30g)
- Onion, 2tbsp (30g)
- Chili flakes, ¼ tsp (1.25)
- Salt, ¼ tsp (1.25g)
- Smoked paprika, ½ tsp (2.5g)
- Thyme, 1 tsp (5g)
- Garlic cloves 2
- Mixed nuts, 1 cup (250g)
- Zucchini roasted, 1 cup (250g)
- Carrots roasted, 1 cup (250g)
- Berries roasted, 1 cup (250)

Procedure

1. One tablespoon of olive oil is heated to medium heat in a pan and soften the onions for 3 minutes.
2. Add the beans, thyme, salt, chili, and smoked paprika. Stir thoroughly, and simmer for additional 8 to 10 minutes while stirring occasionally. Smash half of the beans and add the remaining oil after they are finished.
3. Toast your slices of bread in the meantime in a pan or oven with a little olive oil. Golden brown after a few minutes of cooking.
4. Rub the toasted bread with fresh garlic just before serving, then top with a spoonful of smoky beans, roasted carrots, zucchini, and berries.

Nutrition facts/values (per serving)

Calories – 430kcal | Fat - 2g | Carbs - 30g | Protein - 8g | Sugar – 3g | Fiber – 6g | Potassium - 210mg | Sodium – 299mg | Cholesterol – 0mg

6.8 Nacho Cheesy Chips with Kale and Bell Pepper Board

Preparation Time: 10 min |
Cooking time: 1 hour 30 min | Servings: 10

Ingredients

- Kale, 2 bunches
- Cashews, 2 cups (500g)
- Red bell pepper and Nutritional Yeast, ½ cup (125g)
- Cayenne, salt, and garlic powder, 1 tsp (5g)
- Chili Powder, 2 tbsp (30g)
- Smoke paprika, ½ tsp (2.5g)
- Water, ¾ cup (187.5g)
- Juice of 1 lemon
- Baguette, 1
- Cherries, ¼ cup (62.5g)
- Pickled cucumber, ¼ cup (62.5g)

Procedure

1. Divide the kale into two; you need to be able to toss it around. Add the kale to the bowl.
2. Blend all remaining ingredients in a blender until thoroughly combined. Use your hands to thoroughly coat the kale leaves after adding the "cheese" sauce to them.
3. If you have a dehydrator, set the kale chips in it, and dry them at 120°F (49°C) for 12–14 hours, or until they are crispy. Before serving, let them cool fully.
4. Creating the charcuterie board on a big dish, arrange the ingredients like cheese, pickled cucumber, baguette, and cherries with cheesy Kale chips in the center of the charcuterie board.

Nutrition per Serving:

Calories – 226kcal | Fat - 18g | Carbs - 18g | Protein - 7g | Sugar – 2g | Fiber – 3g | Potassium - 580mg | Sodium – 290mg | Cholesterol – 0mg

6.9 Christmas charcuterie Board

Preparation Time; 10 min |
Cooking time: 10 min | Servings: 15

Ingredients

- Sugar Cookies, 5
- Gingerbread crinkle cookies, 5
- Cookie cake slices, 3
- Cinnamon palm chocolate-covered Oreos, 5
- Graham crackers,
- White chocolate pieces, 4oz (113g)
- Sugared cranberries, 1 cup (100g)
- Candy canes, 7
- Jam, 2 tbsp (30g)
- Sanding sugar, ¼ cup (60g)
- Holiday Marshmallow, 1 cup (250g)
- Frosting, ¼ cup (57g)
- Dried citrus/rosemary for garnish

Procedure

1. Place a cutting board, put sweets, jams, frostings, and sugared cranberries in bowls and platters, and board the ship. Add frosting, sanding sugar, sugared cranberries, jam, add groups of cookies and other larger sweets, cinnamon palmiers, chocolate-covered Oreos, gingerbread crinkle cookies, slices of Christmas cookie cake, cranberry white chocolate shortbread cookies, peppermint white chocolate sugar cookies, sugar cookies.
2. Smaller foods like crackers, marshmallows, and pretzels can be used to fill in any gaps.
3. Graham crackers, candy canes, 1 cup of holiday marshmallows, and white chocolate chunks.
4. Serve after adding any desired garnishes!

Nutrition per Serving:

Calories – 390kcal | Fat - 15g | Carbs - 60g | Protein - 4g | Sugar – 35g | Fiber – 1g | Potassium - 40mg | Sodium – 215mg | Cholesterol – 25mg

6.10 Breakfast Pancake Charcuterie Board

Preparation Time: 20 min |
Cooking time: 40 min | Servings: 10

Ingredients

- Pancake Board; Oil for frying
- Baking soda, salt, vanilla, and baking powder, ½ tsp each.
- Mixed fresh fruits, 3 cups (750g)
- Extra toppings (chocolate chips/coconut/nuts), 1 cup (250g)
- Nutella dip and maple syrup
- Plain flour, 2 cups (500g)
- Sugar, 1 tbsp (15g); Eggs, 2
- Melted butter, 3 tbsp (45g)
- Buttermilk, 2 cups (480ml)

Procedure

1. Grab a board,
2. Make sure all the fruit is sliced, ripe, and ready to eat before preparing it.
3. Make the dips, toppings, and maple syrup. Put into small bowls as necessary.
4. Make crepes, pancakes, etc.
5. Assemble the pancake board. Place the largest pieces first and arrange them artistically on your tray. Group all of your fruit and toppings as you go through them.

Buttermilk Pancakes

1. Flour, salt, sugar, baking powder, and baking soda should all be combined in a mixing dish. To blend, whisk.
2. Put the buttermilk, melted butter, eggs, and vanilla in a jug. Blend by whisking.
3. After adding the buttermilk mixture, carefully fold the dry ingredients into it.
4. In a frying pan, warm a small amount of oil over low heat.
5. Once bubbles appear on the surface of the batter after adding 13 cups (80 ml), flip it over and continue cooking till the other side is golden. Continue until all of the batters have been used.

Nutrition per Serving:

Calories – 280kcal | Fat - 10g | Carbs - 50g | Protein - 5g | Sugar – 17g | Fiber – 3g | Potassium - 210mg | Sodium – 365mg | Cholesterol – 45mg

6.11 Pumpkin Pie Dip Thanksgiving Dessert Board

Preparation Time: 10 min |
Cooking time: 1 hour 10 min | Servings: 3

Ingredients

- Cream cheese, 4oz (60g)
- Powdered sugar, ½ cup (125g)
- Brown sugar, ¼ cup (62.5g)
- Pumpkin Puree, ½ cup (125g)
- Pumpkin spice, 1/2 tbsp (7.5)
- Heavy Whipping Cream, 1 cup (250g)
- Vanilla extract, ½ tsp
- Dried cranberries, ¼ cup (62.5g)
- Mixed nuts, ¼ cup (62.5g)
- Ginger snap cookies and pretzels, 3 each
- Apple and pear slices, ¼ cup (62.5g)
- Pumpkin Pie cheesecake dip, 2tbsp (30g)
- Cinnamon for garnishing

Procedure

1. Chill your mixing bowl and beaters, then whip cold heavy cream, powdered sugar, and vanilla in it until stiff peaks form.
2. Fold ¾ of this whipped cream into the mixed ingredients until smooth, reserving the rest for garnish.
3. Chill the mixture for 30 minutes. On a charcuterie board, place the pumpkin pie dip in the center and arrange apple and pear slices, dried cranberries, mixed nuts, snap cookies, and pretzels around it.
4. Garnish with a sprinkle of cinnamon before serving.

Nutrition per Serving:

Calories – 249kcal | Fat - 11g | Carbs - 45g | Protein - 9g | Sugar – 28g | Fiber – 2.5g | Potassium - 485mg | Sodium – 175mg | Cholesterol – 30mg

6.12 Vegetarian Autumn Cheese Board with Hummus

Preparation Time: 20 min |
Cooking time: 20 min | Servings: 8

Ingredients

- Parmesan, gouda, blue, brie, and goat cheese, 5oz each (150g)
- Crackers, 16
- Bread slices, 8
- Hot chocolate, ¼ cup (62.5g)
- Apple and pear slices, 2 cups (500g)
- Berry or fig jam, 3 tbsp (45g)
- Hummus dip, ½ cup (125g)

Procedure

1. Arrange all of your items on a sizable serving dish, breadboard, or cheeseboard. Serve with your preferred wines.
2. Cherish and have fun.

Nutrition per Serving:

Calories – 130kcal | Fat - 10g | Carbs - 15g | Protein - 4g | Sugar – 14g | Fiber – 2g | Potassium - 75mg | Sodium – 5mg | Cholesterol – 25mg

6.13 Colorful Spring Cheese Board with Candied Meyer Lemons and Lemon Yogurt Dip

Preparation Time: 25 min | Cooking time: 30 min | Servings: 10

Ingredients

- Candied Meyer Lemons
- Meyer Lemons, 4
- Water, 1 cup.
- Sugar, 1 cup (250g)
- Lemon Yogurt Dip
- Plain yogurt, 1 and ½ cups (625g)
- 1 lemon, juice
- Garlic cloves, 5
- Salt and pepper to taste.
- Chives, 2tbsp (30g)
- Basil leaves, 3
- Cheese Board
- Baguette, 2
- Crackers, 10
- Red grapes and strawberries, ½ cup (125g)
- Kiwi, 12 cups (250g)
- Fig Jam, 2tbsp (30g)
- Pickled radish and carrots, ¼ cup
- Olives, ¼ cup (62g)
- Dried apricots and nuts, ½ cup (125g)

Procedure

1. Bring the sugar and water to a boil in a medium saucepan. Until the sugar is entirely dissolved, stir it. Slice the lemons thinly in the meantime.
2. Add the lemon slices to the saucepan and swirl to mix once the sugar has melted.
3. Take the pan off the heat and let the lemons cool in the syrup.
4. The lemons should be carefully removed from the pot, then set on a wire rack to dry. Before serving, transfer to an airtight container and keep in the refrigerator.

LEMON YOGURT DIP

In a small bowl, mix all the ingredients for the yogurt dip. To taste, add salt and pepper to the dish.

CHEESE BOARD

Simply spread out all the ingredients on a sizable cutting board and serve.

Nutrition per Serving:

Calories – 190kcal | Fat - 1g | Carbs - 36g | Protein - 6g | Sugar – 22g | Fiber – 3g | Potassium - 81mg | Sodium – 169mg | Cholesterol – 5mg

6.14 Cinnamon Honey Board with Butter

Preparation Time: 10 min |
Cooking time: 10 min | Servings: 10

Ingredients

- Salted butter, 1 cup (250g)
- Honey, 1/4 cup (62.5g)
- Cinnamon, 1tsp (5g)
- Honeycomb, 1 piece (2inches)
- Bread rolls/Crackers for serving.

Procedure

1. The softened butter, honey, and cinnamon should be thoroughly blended in a mixing dish.
2. A clean serving board should be covered with a single layer of butter.
3. Over the honey, drizzle the remaining honey and top with the final 1/4 teaspoon of cinnamon.
4. Top the butter with the honeycomb, broken into bite-sized pieces (honeycomb is optional).
5. Serve with warm bread, buns, or crackers of your choice.

Nutrition per Serving:

Calories – 190kcal | Fat - 16g | Carbs - 10g | Protein - 1g | Sugar – 6g | Fiber – 0.1g | Potassium - 15mg | Sodium – 150mg | Cholesterol – 30mg

6.15 Rainbow Fruit and Vegetable Charcuterie Board with Kalamata Olives

Preparation Time: 15 min |
Cooking time: 5 min | Servings: 10

Ingredients

- Almonds, ½ cup (125g)
- Vegan feta cheese, ¼ cup (62.5g)
- Green olives, ½ cup (125g)
- Hummus, 1 batch.
- Sliced lemon, 1.
- Kalamata olives, ½ cup (125g)
- Cauliflower, ½ cup
- Egg radishes, 10
- Sliced bell pepper, ½ cup.
- Carrots, 4
- Tomato, 1
- Sugar snap peas and blueberries, ½ cup each (125g)
- Grapefruit wedges, ½
- Few cilantro sprigs and a stalk of celery

Procedure

1. Take a charcuterie-style cutting board. Put each of the following items into a unique dish or plate: green olives, kalamata olives, cauliflower florets, Marcona almonds, vegan feta cheese, hummus, and a garnish of lemon.
2. Spread them out as your "anchors" on the board.
3. You will now begin gathering the sliced fruits and veggies.
4. The Easter egg radishes should be arranged in one corner, going from white to hot pink. Add a layer of sliced yellow, red, and green bell peppers, carrots, tomatoes, celery, sugar snap peas, blueberries, and grapefruit wedges after that.
5. Garnish the dish with cilantro sprigs.

Nutrition per Serving:

Calories – 110 kcal | Fat - 5g | Carbs - 15g | Protein - 3g | Sugar – 6g | Fiber – 3g | Potassium - 325mg | Sodium – 265mg | Cholesterol – 0mg

6.16 Vegetarian Mezze Platter with Sweet Potato Hash Stuffed Portobello Mushrooms

Preparation Time: 15 min |
Cooking time: 15 min | Servings: 4

Ingredients

- Chickpea Hummus, 1 cup (250g)
- Salt and black pepper to taste.
- Falafel, 6-8
- Feta cheese, ½ cup (150g)
- Cucumbers and carrots, 2 each
- Black and green olives, 1 cup (250g)
- Pita chips of your choice
- Portobello Mushrooms, 4
- Extra virgin olive oil, 3tbsp
- Sweet potato, 1
- Chopped Walnuts, ½ cup (125g)
- Red bell pepper, 1
- Water, ¼ cup

Procedure

1. Prepare chickpea hummus and refrigerate. Form falafel balls and chill.
2. Heat oil and fry falafels until golden, then drain. Preheat oven to 425°F.
3. Remove mushroom stems, chop them, and season caps with oil, salt, and pepper; roast for 10-15 minutes. Sauté sweet potato in oil and water, covered for 6-8 minutes.
4. Add bell pepper and mushroom stems, season, and cook for 5 minutes. Stuff mushrooms with this mix, garnish with parsley and walnuts.
5. Serve the falafel, hummus, stuffed mushrooms, and other mezze items together.

Nutrition per Serving:

Calories – 212kcal | Fat - 19g | Carbs - 30g | Protein - 8g | Sugar – 14g | Fiber – 6g | Potassium - 900mg | Sodium – 463mg | Cholesterol – 25mg

6.17 Mexican Inspired Vegetarian Charcuterie Board

Preparation Time: 10 min |
Cooking time: 10 min | Servings: 8

Ingredients

- Minute queso, 5
- Salsa
- Elote corn dip, ¼ cup (62.5g)
- Guacamole, ¼ cup (62.5g)
- Pepper jack cheese/cheddar, 8oz
- Sweet peppers, 1 cup (250g)
- Radish, ¼ cup (62.5g)
- Small avocado, 1
- Mango, 1
- Cucumber, 1
- Tortilla chips

Procedure

1. Start by arranging any products that will be in bowls in a spread-out triangle pattern on the board.
2. Add the cheeses and any large vegetables that have previously been sliced into serving sizes. To make the board more pleasing, arrange them in a triangle around it and place pieces of the same color across from one another.
3. Add the remaining things and continue to fill in the gaps with smaller ones, such as chips, smaller vegetables, almonds, etc. Enjoy after serving!

Nutrition per Serving:

Calories – 240kcal | Fat - 16g | Carbs - 32g | Protein - 5g | Sugar – 8g | Fiber – 7g | Potassium - 500mg | Sodium – 103mg | Cholesterol – 30mg

6.18 Special Charcuterie Board with Baked Tofu

Preparation Time: 15 min |
Cooking time: 15 min | Servings: 12

Ingredients

- Guacamole, ¼ cup (62.5g)
- Baked Tofu, 8oz (240g)
- Mexican street corn, 1 cup (250g)
- Pepper and onion mix, 2 tbsp (30g)
- Tomatoes, ½ cup (125g)
- Colby jack cheese, 8oz (240g)
- Salsa, 4tbsp (30g)
- Tortilla chips
- Sliced jalapenos, 1 cup (250g)
- Shredded purple cabbage, ½ cup (125g)
- Red cabbage, ½ cup (125g)

Procedure

1. In the center of the board, layer the purple cabbage shreds in a circle.
2. Place tiny bowls filled with ingredients such as salsa, guacamole, street corn, cheese, and chopped cilantro around the board's perimeter.
3. Prepare baked tofu, then top the red cabbage and tomatoes in the middle of the board with a scoop.

Nutrition per Serving:

Calories – 140kcal | Fat - 10g | Carbs - 12g | Protein - 8g | Sugar – 2g | Fiber – 4g | Potassium - 405mg | Sodium – 395mg | Cholesterol – 25mg

6.19 Halloween Charcuterie Board

Preparation Time: 20 min |
Cooking time: 10 min | Servings: 10

Ingredients

- Tofu, 2 cups (500g)
- Bright orange colored cheese, 3 cups
- Assorted crackers, 12oz
- Fruits, veggies, and pickles, 1 and ½ cups
- Mixed nuts and chia seeds, ¾ cup
- Halloween treats like pumpkin cakes, ghost cookies, and candy corn, 12oz.
- Jam/ Honey, 4tbsp (60g)
- Small Halloween decoration spiders
- Fresh herbs

Procedure

1. The cheese, jam, and bowls of pickles should all be placed on a large platter.
2. Crackers, fruit, and vegetables should then be added to the board.
3. The platter should now include meats and Halloween sweets.
4. Nuts and seeds can fill any space.
5. Fresh herbs should be used as a garnish. Serve with little Halloween decorations.

Nutrition per Serving:

Calories – 290kcal | Fat - 20g | Carbs - 12g | Protein - 15g | Sugar – 4g | Fiber – 3g | Potassium - 175mg | Sodium – 510mg | Cholesterol – 30mg

6.20 Caramel Apple Charcuterie Board

Preparation Time: 20 min |
Cooking time: 20 min | Servings: 8

Ingredients

- Apples of different varieties, 4
- Sprite Bottle, 12oz
- Lollipop sticks, 1 package.
- Caramel, 1 cup.
- White and milk chocolate wafers, ½ cup each
- Toppings
- Gummy bears, 2 tbsp
- Crushed Oreos, ½ cup
- Heath bar bits, 2 tbsp
- Trail mix cereals, ½ cup
- Diced candy bars and nuts, ½ cup.
- Cinnamon sugar, 1 tbsp

Procedure

1. Apples should be cored, quartered, and seedless. Pour the Sprite into a small dish to keep the apples from browning. After dipping the apples, place the bowl aside.
2. With a lollipop stick, pierce each apple wedge.
3. Separate small bowls should be used for the various toppings and caramel sauce.
4. The white chocolate melts should be added to a bowl that can go in the microwave and melted as directed on the container.
5. Allow everyone to dip their apples in the caramel, chocolate, and toppings after adding the apple slices to the board.

Nutrition per Serving:

Calories – 240kcal | Fat - 8g | Carbs - 39g | Protein - 3g | Sugar – 34g | Fiber – 3g | Potassium - 120mg | Sodium – 72mg | Cholesterol – 7mg

6.21 Ultimate Crudite Charcuterie Board

Preparation Time: 20 min |
Cooking time: 20 min | Servings: 8

Ingredients

- Marinated feta, 8 oz
- Sundried tomatoes, 8
- Peppercorns, 4
- Extra virgin olive oil, 2 tbsp (60g)
- Garlic cloves, 2
- Fresh thyme, 6 sprigs
- Tart Cherry Thyme Butter
- Unsalted butter, ½ cup (125g)
- Honey, 1 and ½ tsp (7.5g)
- Dried tart cherries, 1 and ½ tsp (7.5g)

Herby White Bean Dip

- Olive oil, basil leaves, and lemon juice, 2 tbsp each (30g each)
- Rosemary, lemon zest, black pepper, and sea salt, ½ tsp each (2.5g each)
- Water, ¼ cup (62.5g)

For Serving

- Sliced cucumbers, 2.
- Rainbow carrots, 3
- Tomatoes, 2
- Snap peas, 1 and ½ cups.
- Baguette, 1

Procedure

1. To make marinated feta, layer thyme, sun-dried tomatoes, feta, peppercorns, and garlic in a jar and cover with olive oil. For Cherry Thyme Butter, blend butter, dried cherries, thyme, honey, and salt in a food processor until smooth, then transfer to a serving plate.
2. Prepare white bean dip by processing cannellini beans with olive oil, basil, thyme, rosemary, lemon juice, and zest.
3. Arrange the marinated feta, cherry butter, and white bean dip on a platter with sliced cucumbers, snap peas, carrots, tomatoes, and baguette slices for serving.

Nutrition per Serving:

Calories – 198kcal | Fat - 8g | Carbs - 11g | Protein - 3g | Sugar – 7g | Fiber – 4g | Potassium - 313mg | Sodium – 218mg | Cholesterol – 15mg

6.22 Falafel Mezze Platter with Tahini Sauce

Preparation Time: 30 min |
Cooking time: 20 min | Servings: 4

Ingredients/ Food List

- Dried chickpeas, 2 cups (500g)
- Garlic cloves, 4
- Chopped onion, 1.
- Chopped parsley, ½ cup (125g)
- Broccoli, 1 cup (250g)
- Fresh Coriander, ¾ cup
- Coriander, cumin, salt, and black pepper, 1 tsp each (5g each)

Mezze Platter

- Falafel, 12
- Potatoes and carrots, 2 each
- Hummus, 1 cup (250g)
- Cucumber, ½
- Cherry Tomatoes, 7-8
- Olive oil, 1tbsp (15g)
- Halloumi, 1 block.
- Aubergine, ½
- Zucchini, 1
- Roasted/Grilled veggies, 1 cup.
- Pita Bread

Tahini Sauce

- Tahini, ¼ cup
- Water, 1/3 cup.
- Lemon juice, 2tbap
- Salt to taste

Procedure

1. Combine tahini, water, and lemon juice to produce the tahini sauce easily. Until the mixture has a creamy texture, thoroughly combine all the components.
2. At least 12 hours should pass after the chickpeas have soaked before making falafels.
3. Rinse your chickpeas and drain the extra water after soaking them for at least 12 hours. They should be added and blended briefly in a food processor.
4. Add the onion, broccoli, coriander, parsley, cumin powder, black pepper, and salt to the food processor.
5. When you have a consistent dough, combine all the ingredients.
6. Round out the dough by forming it with your hands or a falafel press. It needs to be roughly palm-sized. The falafels should be fried until the outside is crispy and brown.
7. Bake some potato chips and carrot slices on a baking sheet while the oven is preheated at 180°C. Salt and some olive oil should be added for 25 to 30 minutes before baking.
8. Cucumber and cherry tomatoes should be finely chopped before being combined with extra virgin olive oil and salt.
9. Halloumi, sliced aubergine, and sliced zucchini are grilled on a griddle pan with some heated oil.
10. Pita bread should be warmed before serving with the mezze platter.

Nutrition per Serving:

Calories – 740kcal | Fat - 33g | Carbs - 109g | Protein - 26g | Sugar – 20g | Fiber – 19g | Potassium - 2156mg | Sodium – 901mg | Cholesterol – 20mg

6.23 Spicy Vegan Charcuterie Board

Preparation time: 10 mins |
Cooking time: 10 mins | Servings: 6

Ingredients

- Broccoli, 1 cup (250g)
- Cherry tomatoes, 1 cup (250g)
- Asparagus, 20 spears
- Sliced carrots, 1 cup (250g)
- Sliced Zucchini, 1 cup (250g)
- Crimini mushroom, 20 whole
- Tortilla chips, 1 cup (250g)
- Potato chips, 1 cup (250g)
- Tomato Marinara, 1 cup (250g)
- Spicy cilantro cream sauce, 1 cup (250g)
- Vegan cheese fondue dip, 1 cup (250g)
- Crispy chickpeas, 1 cup (150g)
- Cashews and dried apricots, 1 cup (175g)

Procedure

1. Mix thoroughly black pepper and honey in a bowl. Place it in one corner of the board.
2. Start with the larger items, such as cheeses, and place them in the spotlight.
3. Place bowls of your dips along the outside of the snack board space.
4. Next, place your larger vegetables, bread, etc. between the cheeses and dips.
5. Next, fill in the biggest objects.
6. Start with little items that can be heaped up and distributed, such as nuts and dried fruit, to fill in any gaps.

Nutrition per Serving:

Calories – 750kcal | Fat - 35g | Carbs - 101g | Protein - 25g | Sugar – 26g | Fiber – 16g | Potassium - 1172mg | Sodium – 1072mg | Cholesterol – 0mg

6.24 Mediterranean Cudites Board with Tzatziki Sauce

Preparation time: 20 mins |
Cooking time: 10 mins | Servings: 10

Ingredients

- Cooked beets, 1 cup (250g)
- Snap peas, 1 cup (250g)
- Radishes, 1 cup (250g)
- Tzatziki, 1 cup (250g)
- Walnut-Spinach Yogurt dip, 1 cup (250g)
- Marinated Artichoke hearts, ½ cup (125g)
- Green olives, ½ cup (125g)
- Bell peppers, 1 cup (250g)
- Marinated feta, 1 cup (250g)
- Pita Bread wedges

Procedure

1. Place a small dish of tzatziki sauce on one side of a sizable platter or board. If you're using two dips, place the two bowls on the platter on the opposing sides.
2. Fill in the spaces surrounding the dip with the vegetables as you arrange them on the platter. Use vegetables that are distinct in color and texture close to one another to create a stunning platter by separating those with similar colors.
3. The remaining components, which include olives, grapes, cheese feta, and pita wedges, should fill in any spaces on your platter.

Nutrition per Serving:

Calories – 150kcal | Fat - 5g | Carbs - 90g | Protein - 8g | Sugar – 9g | Fiber – 8g | Potassium - 205mg | Sodium – 450mg | Cholesterol – 8mg

6.25 Vegan Grazing Charcuterie Board

Preparation time: 15 mins |
Cooking time: 0 mins | Servings: 8

Ingredients

- Quinoa tabbouleh salad, 1 cup (250g)
- Sliced cucumber, 1.
- Roasted red pepper hummus, 1 and ½ cups (375g)
- Wheat crackers, 16
- Pomegranate arils, 1 cup (250g)
- Kalamata olives, ½ cup (125g)
- Olive tapenade, 19oz
- Quick pickled red onions, 1 cup (250g)
- Capers, ¼ cup (62.5g)
- Figs halved, 10.
- Fresh mint leaves for garnish

Procedure

1. Position the medium bowl of the quinoa tabbouleh salad adjacent to the board's left centre. Spread the cucumber all around the tabbouleh.
2. Set the tiny bowl of Roasted Red Pepper Hummus on the board's opposite side. The bowl is covered in wheat crackers.
3. Arrange the pomegranate arils, capers, olive tapenade, pickled onions, olives, and figs on the board in small bowls.
4. Add fresh mint leaves as a garnish and serve the board.

Nutrition per Serving:

Calories – 541kcal | Fat - 15g | Carbs - 95g | Protein - 11g | Sugar – 36g | Fiber – 14g | Potassium - 1220mg | Sodium – 1023mg | Cholesterol – 0mg

6.26 Fruicuterie Board

Preparation time: 20 mins |
Cooking time: 0 mins | Servings: 16

Ingredients

- Aged goat cheese, 4oz (120g)
- Brie cheese, 4oz (120g)
- Soft triple cream cheese, 4oz (120g)
- Sliced kiwis, 3.
- Diced mangoes, 3.
- Grapes, 4 bunches
- Cherries, 4 handfuls
- Figs halved, 6.
- Sliced peaches, 2.
- Sliced apricots, 3.
- Sliced plums, 3.
- Cubed cantaloupe, 1 cup (250g)
- Strawberries, 1 cup (250g)
- Raspberries, 1 cup (250g)

Procedure

1. Mix thoroughly black pepper and honey in a bowl. Place it in one corner of the board.
2. The cheese should be spread out on a sizable dish and let soften for 20 to 30 minutes at room temperature. Around the cheese, group the fruit in clusters.

Nutrition per Serving:

Calories – 190kcal | Fat - 9g | Carbs - 25g | Protein - 10g | Sugar – 18g | Fiber – 3g | Potassium - 216mg | Sodium – 150mg | Cholesterol – 30mg

6.27 Simple Flatbreads Charcuterie Board

Preparation time: 20 mins |
Cooking time: 0 mins | Servings: 4

Ingredients

- Tapenade, ¼ cup (250g)
- Toasted flatbread, 2 pieces
- Tofu, 16oz
- Pistachios, 2 tbsp (30g)
- Burrata, 4oz
- Raw honey
- Crushed red pepper flakes.

Procedure

1. Mix thoroughly black pepper and honey in a bowl. Place it in one corner of the board.
2. Each slice of flatbread should have 2 teaspoons of tapenade spread on it before prosciutto is added. Add a spoonful of burrata to each. and some pistachios on top.
3. If using, top each flatbread with honey and a sprinkle of crushed red pepper flakes.

Nutrition per Serving:

Calories – 325kcal | Fat - 24g | Carbs - 15g | Protein - 13g | Sugar – 2g | Fiber – 2g | Potassium - 146mg | Sodium – 378mg | Cholesterol – 20mg

6.28 Butternut Squash Cheeseball Board

Preparation time: 20 mins |
Cooking time: 0 mins | Servings: 4

Ingredients

- Butternut Squash, 1 cup (250g)
- Brown butter, 2 tbsp (30g)
- Olive oil, 1 tbsp (15g)
- Fresh sage, 1 handful
- Soft cream cheese, 4oz (120g)
- Parmesan cheese, 2/3 cup.
- Salt and black pepper, ¼ tsp each (5g each)
- Grated nutmeg, 1/8 tsp (2g)
- Hot capicola, 1 cup (250g)
- Marinated olives, ½ cup (125g)
- Pumpkin seed salsa and pomegranate arils, 1/3 cup each (50g)
- Whole grain mustard, ¼ cup (62.5g)
- Cornichons, ¼ cup (62.5g)
- Red seedless grapes, 2 bunches
- Whole grain crackers

Procedure

1. You should put squash cubes in a pot with cold water. After bringing it to a boil over high heat, reduce the heat to a simmer. Simmer the cubes for 15 to 20 minutes, or until they are tender to the fork. Drain all of the water from them.
2. Warm the olives and fresh sage.
3. Combine the cooked butternut squash, brown butter, crispy sage, cream cheese, parmesan, salt, nutmeg, and pepper in a food processor.
4. Scoop it out onto a piece of plastic wrap until it is smooth. Make a ball out of it, then securely wrap it. Put it in the refrigerator for at least 30 minutes.
5. Put the chopped walnuts on a platter after 30 minutes. The cheeseball should be taken out of the fridge and placed on the chopped walnuts. Put walnuts on the ball. Serve the board with cheeseballs.

Nutrition per Serving:

Calories – 229kcal | Fat - 17g | Carbs - 19g | Protein - 4g | Sugar – 1g | Fiber – 2.8g | Potassium - 160mg | Sodium – 319mg | Cholesterol – 25mg

6.29 Brunch Board

Preparation time: 30 mins |
Cooking time: 0 mins | Servings: 4

Ingredients

- Pancakes, 4 cup (250g)
- Eggs, 2
- Pancakes, 4
- Cheddar cheese, 4oz (120g)
- Crispy chickpeas, 1 cup (250g)
- Tofu, 8 oz (240g)
- Mixed carrots, radish, broccoli, and cucumbers, 1 cup (250g)
- Blueberries, pineapple, and watermelon, 1 cup (250g)
- Walnuts and pecans halves, 8

Procedure

1. Arrange the pancakes or waffles on a wooden board.
2. Position the cheeses and meats all over the waffles.
3. Fill in any gaps with nuts, fruits, and veggies. Use little dishes or cups to add more depth. For a splash of color, garnish with flowers and fresh herbs. Enjoy

Nutrition per Serving:

Calories – 302kcal | Fat - 22g | Carbs - 15g | Protein - 11g | Sugar – 12g | Fiber – 3.5g | Potassium - 721mg | Sodium – 546mg | Cholesterol – 55mg

6.30 Breakfast Waffle Charcuterie Board

Preparation time: 15 mins |
Cooking time: 10 mins | Servings: 4

Ingredients

- Blue berry waffles, 1 cup (250g)
- Blueberries, ½ cup (125g)
- Bananas, grapes, and strawberries, ¼ cup each (62.5g)
- Granola, 2/3 cup (70g)
- Nutella, 4tbsp (60g)
- Yogurt, ¾ cup (175g)
- Whipped cream, ¼ cup (62.5g)

Procedure

1. Prepare and wash all of your fruits.
2. Prepare your toppings by arranging them in separate dishes and setting them aside.
3. When the waffles are finished, break them into pieces and arrange them in a beautiful manner on a 12 × 18-inch (or comparable) charcuterie board. Be inventive!
4. Next, distribute all of the prepared toppings across the waffles.
5. Finalize your morning charcuterie board by gently filling the remaining empty spots with all of the previously prepared fruits.
6. Serve and delight!

Nutrition per Serving::

Calories: 240kcal | Fat: 8g | Carbs: 37g | Protein: 6g | Sugar: 14g | Fiber: 4.5g | Potassium: 260mg | Sodium: 222mg | Cholesterol: 10mg

7 VEGAN CHARCUTERIE BOARDS

7.1 Vegan board

Preparation time: 15 mins |
Cooking time: 10 mins | Servings: 8

Ingredients

Vegetarian meats

- Veggie Sausages Tuscan, 3 oz (90g)
- Harmless Ham, 3 oz (90g)

Dips

- Vegan cheese produced at home or bought from a store, 2 oz (60g)
- Hummus, ½ cup (125g)
- Jam or jellies, ½ cup (125g)

Fruits

- Purple or green grapes, 2 pound (907g)
- Fresh cranberries, ½ cup (125g)
- Olives, 1 cup (250g)

Vegetables

- Carrots, cut into sticks after being sliced, 1 cup (250g)
- Celery stalks, cut into sticks after being sliced, 1 cup (250g)
- Sliced bell pepper, ½ cup (125g)

Other

- Whole-wheat crackers, 3 oz (100g)
- Mixed nuts, 1 cup (250g)
- For garnish, use fresh rosemary.

Procedure

1. Veggie sausages should be prepared as directed on the packaging. On a sizable serving platter, arrange slices of vegetable ham and sausages.
2. Put jam, hummus, and vegan cheese in separate small bowls. Set on a serving tray.
3. On the serving platter, arrange the fruit, veg, crackers, almonds, and rosemary.

Nutrition per Serving:

Calories: 369 | Fat: 6g | Carbs: 12g | Protein: 8g | Sugar: 6g | Fiber: 5g | Potassium: 902mg | Sodium: 1209mg | Cholesterol: 0mg

7.2 Avocado charcuterie board

Preparation time: 20 mins |
Cooking time: 0 mins | Servings: 10

Ingredients

- Avocado dip 1 cup (250g)
- Bell peppers, 1 cup (250g)
- Baked tortilla chips, 2 cup (500g)
- Roasted red peppers, 7 ounces (1750g)
- Lime slices, 4
- Cherry tomatoes, 1 cup (250g)
- Watermelon, ½ cup (125g)
- Cilantro ½ cup (125g)

Procedure

1. Spoon the dip or guacamole into a medium serving bowl. Lime wedges can be used as a garnish, if preferred. Place the bowl close to the center of the board.
2. Cover all four corners of the board with a layer of tortilla chips and bell pepper halves.
3. Arrange the cheese slices, pepper halves, and chips on the board in three separate groups. On one of the board's open corners, put a small bowl with roasted red pepper slices.
4. Position pieces of mango on either side of the dipping bowl. Decorate the board with cilantro sprigs.

Nutrition per Serving:

Calories: 130 | Fat: 5g | Carbs: 3g | Protein: 2g | Sugar: 2g | Fiber: 3g | Potassium: 480mg | Sodium: 981mg | Cholesterol: 0mg

7.3 Appetizer board with pickle

Preparation time: 40 mins |
Cooking time: 0 mins | Servings: 16

Ingredients

- Mixed vegetables 2 cup (500g)
- White vinegar, 2 cup (500g)
- Cups of water, 1 cup (250g0
- Sugar, 1 ½ tsp (7.5g)
- Salt, ½ tsp (2.5g)
- Dill, fresh, 3 sprigs
- Seeds of mustard, 1 tsp (5g)
- Coriander seeds 1 tsp (5g)
- Black peppercorns, 1 tsp (5g)

Appetizer board

- Board plain skiers, 1 cup (250g)
- Pickles, ½ cup (125g)
- Cucumbers, ½ (125g)
- Medium tomatoes, 2
- Capers, three tbsp.
- Lemon wedges,
- Salt, and black pepper to taste.
- Rye toasted, 4 oz (120g)

Procedure

1. Slice the vegetables, then pack them tightly into jars to make pickles. Mix the dill, coriander, mustard seeds, peppercorns, vinegar, water, sugar, salt and sugar in a medium pot. Over medium-high heat, boil gently for about 4 minutes. Over the vegetables, pour the brine. Give it an hour to reach room temperature. Before serving, put in the refrigerator for at least 24 hours.
2. Place a bowl on a sizable platter or board. The dish should be topped with the pickles, rye toast, cucumber, tomatoes, capers, and lemon wedges.

Nutrition per Serving:

Calories: 170 | Fat: 5g | Carbs: 2g | Protein: 8g | Sugar: 1g | Fiber: 2g | Potassium: 891mg | Sodium: 719mg | Cholesterol: 0mg

7.4 Salad board appetizer

Preparation time: 45 mins |
Cooking time: 0 mins | Servings: 6

Ingredients

- Hummus, ½ cup (125g)
- Olive oil Dressing
- Black Pepper; and Salt, each 1/2 tsp (2.5g)
- Honey, 1 tsp (5g)
- Garlic clove, 2
- Lemon juice, 2 tsp (10g)

Marinated apple

- Small apples, 2 cup (500g0
- White vinegar, 1 ½ tbsp. (22.5g)
- Fresh parsley, 2 tbsp (30g)
- Small onion, ½ cup (125g)
- Salt, ½ tsp (2.5g)

Salad Plate

- Mixed salad greens, 1 cup (250g)
- Cherry tomatoes, ½ cup (125g)
- String beans, 7 oz (210)
- Carrot, ½ cup (125g)
- Medium avocado, 1 cup (250g)

Procedure

1. First, prepare the lemon juice, scallions, garlic, mustard, honey, ½ teaspoon salt, and pepper should all be combined in a small basin.
2. To make the marinated apples, combine the parsley, vinegar,, shallot, apple and salt in a medium bowl. Set aside to marinate, stirring periodically.
3. Organizing the salad board Combine the corn and greens in separate bowls. The bowls should be arranged in a row on a large plate or tray. For the peaches, place a second bowl on the board. Place the dressing on the board after pouring it into a little jar.
4. Arrange the bowls with the goat cheese, radish, beans, cucumbers, tomatoes and avocado. The apple should then be placed in the last bowl.

Nutrition per Serving:

Calories – 671 | Fat - 32g | Carbs - 40g | Protein - 22g | Sugar – 10g | Fiber – 7g | Potassium - 571mg | Sodium – 905mg | Cholesterol – 0mg

7.5 Roasted green grapes board.

Preparation time: 20 mins |
Cooking time: 0 mins | Servings: 6

Ingredients

- Green grapes, 1 cup (250g)
- Olive oil, 2 tbsp (30g)
- Each spring of thyme and rosemary, 5
- Figs, ½ cup (125g)
- Smoked almonds, ½ cup (125)
- Crackers, and sliced baguette

Procedure

1. Preheat the oven to 450°F (230°C), meanwhile place parchment paper on baking sheet.
2. Arrange grape bunches on the baking sheet. Olive oil, salt, and pepper should all be combined with the grapes in a bowl. Place the grapes in between the thyme and rosemary.
3. Roast the grapes for 12 to 15 minutes. Grapes should be placed in the centre of a broad board. The grapes should be surrounded with almonds and figs. Serve with baguette and crackers.

Nutrition per Serving:

Calories – 731 | Fat - 5g | Carbs - 30g | Protein - 2g | Sugar – 24g | Fiber – 3g | Potassium - 1459mg | Sodium – 1390mg | Cholesterol – 0mg

7.6 Smoked beans with vegan charcuterie board.

Preparation time: 5 mins |
Cooking time: 10 mins | Servings: 10

Ingredients

- Slices of toasted bread, 12 (60g)
- Drained beans, 14 oz (420g)
- Virgin olive oil, 2 tbsp (30g)
- Small Onion, ½ cup (125g)
- Chili flakes, ¼ teaspoon (1.25g)
- Salt, ¼ tsp (1.25g)
- Smoked paprika, ½ tsp (2.5g)
- Thyme, 1 tsp (5g)
- Garlic cloves, 3
- Mixed nuts, ½ cup (125g)
- Roasted cucumber ½ cup (125g)
- Roasted carrots, 1 cup (250)
- Roasted berries, ½ cup (250)

Procedure

1. For the first step, heat one tablespoon of olive oil in a pan over medium heat for three minutes to soften the onions.
2. Add salt, smoked paprika, chili, thyme, and beans. Mix completely, then simmer for a further 8 to 10 minutes while stirring once and then. After they are done, smash half of the beans and add the remaining oil.
3. While you wait, toast your bread slices in a pan or oven with a small quantity of olive oil. After a few minutes of cooking, it is golden brown.
4. Just before serving, rub fresh garlic on the toast. Add a dollop of smoked beans, roasted carrots, zucchini, and berries on top.

Nutrition per Serving:

Calories – 561 | Fat - 20g | Carbs - 42g | Protein - 41g | Sugar – 6g | Fiber – 8g | Potassium - 182mg | Sodium – 152mg | Cholesterol – 0mg

7.7 Cashews and bell pepper board

Preparation time: 20 mins |
Cooking time: 0 mins | Servings: 6

Ingredients

- Collard green, 3 bunches
- Cashews, 1 cup (250g)
- Nutritional yeast, ½ cup (125g)
- Orange bell pepper, 1 cup (250g)
- Cayenne, salt, and garlic powder, ½ tsp of each (2.5g)
- Chili powder, 1 ½ tbsp. (7.5g)
- Smoke paprika, 1 tsp (2.5g)
- Water, 1 cup (250g)
- Lemon juice, 2 tsp (10g)
- Cherries, ½ cup (125g)
- Pickled celery, ½ cup (125g)

Procedure

1. Split the kale in half; it must be able to be tossed. To the bowl, add the greens.
2. Use a blender to incorporate all remaining ingredients completely. After pouring the kale leaves, thoroughly coat them with your hands.
3. Place the kale chips in a dehydrator if you have one and dry them at 120°F (50°C) for 12 to 14 hours, or until they are crisp. To serve, allow them too completely cool.
4. Making the charcuterie board, fourth Place the charcuterie board's items, such as pickled cucumber, baguette, and cherries, in the center of a large dish.

Nutrition per Serving:

Calories – 561 | Fat - 47g | Carbs - 32g | Protein - 14g | Sugar – 6g | Fiber – 5g | Potassium - 1952mg | Sodium – 852mg | Cholesterol – 0mg

7.8 Pancake charcuterie board for breakfast

Preparation time: 10 mins |
Cooking time: 15 mins | Servings: 4

Ingredients

- Flour, 2 cup (500g)
- Natural sweetener, 4tsp (20g)
- Baking soda, 2tsp (10g)
- Salt, 1 tsp (5g)
- Almond milk, 2 cup (250g)
- Vinegar made from apple cider, 2 tsp (10g)
- Maple syrup with vanilla, to be served, 2 tsp (10g)

Procedure

1. In a larger basin, combine the salt, baking soda, sugar, and flour.
2. In a medium bowl or liquid measuring cup, combine the almond milk, apple cider vinegar, and vanilla.
3. Combine both mixtures. (liquid and dry mixtures).
4. Allow the batter to rest for only 05 minutes long.
5. Using a nonstick griddle or skillet over medium heat, pour the batter.
6. When the top of the pancake begins to bubble, flip it over and cook it until it turns to golden color.
7. Add warm maple syrup in the last step.

Nutrition per Serving:

Calories – 157 | Fat - 1g | Carbs - 32g | Protein - 3g | Sugar – 4g | Fiber – 1g | Potassium - 402mg | Sodium – 201mg | Cholesterol – 0mg

7.9 Vegan pancake board

Preparation time: 5 mins |
Cooking time: 10 mins | Servings: 3

Ingredients

- All-purpose flour, 3 cups (750g)
- White sugar, 4 tbsp (60g)
- Baking powder, 4 tbsp (60g)
- Salt, 1 tsp (5g)
- Water, ½ cup (125g)
- Oil, 2 tsp (10g)

Procedure

1. To form a well in the center, sift salt, baking soda, sugar, and flour into a large bowl. In a separate bowl, whisk the water and oil; add to the flour mixture. The mixture will be lumpy; stir only until combined.
2. An oiled griddle is heated to medium-high heat.
3. Pour batter onto the griddle in generous spoonful. Until bubbles appear and the edges are dry, cook. After flipping, heat for 1–2 minutes, or until its bottoms change color to brown. Use the leftover batter to repeat.

Nutrition per Serving:

Calories – 264 | Fat - 5g | Carbs - 49g | Protein - 5g | Sugar – 9g | Fiber – 2g | Potassium - 58mg | Sodium – 717mg | Cholesterol – 0mg

7.10 Pancakes special board

Preparation time: 10mins |
Cooking time: 10 mins | Servings: 8

Ingredients

- Flour, 2 cup (500g)
- Rolled oats, 12 tbsp (180g)
- Baking soda, ¼ tsp (1.25g)
- Baking powder, 5 tsp (25g)
- Salt, 1 tsp (5g)
- Almond milk or water, 1 cup (250g)
- White or cider vinegar, 4 tsp (20g)
- Oil, nut butter, 2 tbsp (30g)
- Sweetener of choice, 4 tbsp (20g)

Procedure

1. Take a bowl and mix dry ingredients, then stir in the other ingredients to make the pancakes. Let the mixture sit for 10 minutes to thicken if you want extra fluffy pancakes. You can also omit this step and simply add more liquid to the batter to thin it out if you want thinner pancakes. Add more water until you have a batter consistency—some flour will require more water than others.
2. In a non-stick skillet, liberally grease the pan and heat. Drop tiny ladles of batter into the pan and push down once it is heated.
3. The edges of the pancakes will be done before the center are cooked if you make them too large. Each pancake can optionally have some berries, banana slices, or chocolate chips added. Flip with a spatula when edges start to seem dry. Before taking them off the heat, give them one or two more minutes to cook. To avoid sticking, oil the skillet again after each batch of pancakes. You can prepare the batter the night before and store it in the fridge in a covered bowl to save time in the morning. Or you may freeze any leftover pancakes and thaw them later to enjoy them.

Nutrition per Serving:

Calories – 781 | Fat - 5g | Carbs - 12g | Protein - 7g | Sugar – 4g | Fiber – 3g | Potassium - 1892mg | Sodium – 721mg | Cholesterol – 0mg

7.11 Hummus and vegan board

Preparation time: 0 mins |
Cooking time: 0 mins | Servings: 5

Ingredients

- Crackers, 15
- Slices of bread, 9 (45g)
- Hot chocolate, ½ cup (125g0
- Pear and guava slices, 1 cup (250g)
- Berry jam, 4 tbsp (60g)
- Hummus dip, 1 cup (250)

Procedure

1. Spread out all of your ingredients on a sizable serving platter, cheeseboard, or breadboard. Serve alongside your favorite wines.
2. Enjoy and cherish.

Nutrition per Serving:

Calories – 561 | Fat - 20g | Carbs - 31g | Protein - 5g | Sugar – 5g | Fiber – 3g | Potassium - 1902mg | Sodium – 189mg | Cholesterol – 0mg

7.12 Charcuterie board with cinnamon

Preparation time: 10 mins |
Cooking time: 0 mins | Servings: 4

Ingredients

- Honey, ½ cup (125g)
- Cinnamon, 2 tsp (10g)
- Honeycomb, 2 pieces
- Mango, 3 oz (100g)
- Bread rolls or crackers, 3 oz (100g)

Procedure

1. In a bowl, combine the honey, and cinnamon completely.
2. Drizzle the remaining honey over the honey and sprinkle the remaining cinnamon on top.
3. Place the honeycomb, broken into bite-sized pieces. Place mango slices.
4. Serve with your preferred warm bread, buns, or crackers.

Nutrition per Serving:

Calories – 211 | Fat - 3g | Carbs - 50g | Protein - 6g | Sugar – 43g | Fiber – 1g | Potassium - 1390mg | Sodium – 290mg | Cholesterol – 0mg

7.13 Guacomole board

Preparation time: 15 mins |
Cooking time: 0 mins | Servings: 4

Ingredients

- Salsa
- Corn dip, ½ cup (125g)
- Guacamole, ½ cup (125g)
- Green peppers, 2 cup (500g)
- Radish, ½ cup
- Carrot, ½ cup
- Medium avocado, 1
- Papaya, 1 cup (250g)
- Cucumber, 2
- Tortilla chips, 1 bag.

Procedure

1. Begin by spreading out any items that will be placed in bowls in a triangle arrangement on the board.
2. Include any large veggies that have already been cut into serving-size pieces. Place pieces of the same color across from one another to add aesthetic appeal to the board by arranging them in a triangle around it.
3. Continue to fill in the spaces with smaller items, such as chips, smaller vegetables, nuts, papaya etc., and then add the remaining ingredients. After serving, delight.

Nutrition per Serving:

Calories – 147 | Fat - 20g | Carbs - 30g | Protein - 4g | Sugar – 6g | Fiber – 9g | Potassium - 781mg | Sodium – 128mg | Cholesterol – 0mg

7.14 Cherish charcuterie board

Preparation time: 15 mins |
Cooking time: 0 mins | Servings: 6

Ingredients

- Tofu, 1 cup (250g)
- Fruits, vegetables, pickles, 1 cups (250g)
- Assorted crackers, 6 oz (180g)
- Mixed nuts, ½ cup (125g)
- Pumpkin cakes, 1
- Cookies, 6
- jam or honey, ½ cup (125g)
- Fresh herbs

Procedure

1. A big plate should hold the jam, honey, and bowls of pickles.
2. After that, add crackers, produce, and veggies to the board. Place pumpkin cake.
3. Any void can be filled with nuts and seeds.
4. You should garnish it with fresh herbs. Add a few decorations before serving.

Nutrition per Serving:

Calories – 180 | Fat - 4g | Carbs - 16g | Protein - 7g | Sugar – 10g | Fiber – 3g | Potassium - 236mg | Sodium – 189mg | Cholesterol – 0mg

7.15 Recipes for a vegan snack board

Preparation time: 15 mins |
Cooking time: 0 mins | Servings: 6

Ingredients

- White quinoa, 1 cup (250g)
- Water, 2 cup (500g)
- Freshly chopped curly parsley, 2 bunches
- Finely chopped fresh mint leaves, ½ cup (125g)
- Quartered grape tomatoes, 16 oz (480g)
- Scallions finally chopped, 4.
- Olive oil, 4tsp (20g)
- Lemon juice, 2 tablespoon (30g)
- Chopped garlic clove, 2.
- Salt, ½ tsp (2.5g)
- A few black peppercorns

Procedure

1. In a saucepan, combine the quinoa and water, and heat until boiling. Low heat is applied while the pot is covered.
2. The quinoa should be simmered for 10 minutes or until it has absorbed all of the water. With a fork, fluff the quinoa after taking it off the heat. Set apart for cooling.
3. Place the tomatoes, scallions, mint, parsley, and mint in a serving bowl.
4. To make the dressing, combine the black pepper, garlic, salt, lemon juice, and olive oil in a small container. Fasten the cover firmly and vigorously shake to combine the ingredients.

Nutrition per Serving:

Calories – 135 | Fat - 3g | Carbs - 25g | Protein - 5g | Sugar – 3g | Fiber – 4g | Potassium - 631mg | Sodium – 172mg | Cholesterol – 0mg

7.16 Hummus with roasted pepper

Preparation time: 20 mins | Cooking time: 0 mins | Servings: 6

Ingredients

- Can have rinsed and drained chickpeas, 2 can.
- Coarsely chopped roasted red peppers, 1 cup (250g)
- Tahini, 4 tbsp (60g)
- Lemon juice, 4 tsp (20g)
- Garlic clove, coarsely diced, 2.
- Salt, 1 tsp (5g)
- Olive oil, 2 tsp (10g)

Procedure

1. Combine the salt, garlic, lemon juice, tahini, red peppers and chickpeas in a food processor's bowl.
2. Slowly pour the olive oil through the top while operating the food processor. For about a minute, blend the hummus until it is perfectly smooth. If necessary, add another pinch of salt after tasting.
3. To serve the hummus on the Board, scoop it into a bowl, cover it, and chill.

Nutrition per Serving:

Calories – 450 | Fat - 12g | Carbs - 45g | Protein - 7g | Sugar – 5g | Fiber – 10g | Potassium - 237mg | Sodium – 1348mg | Cholesterol – 0mg

7.17 Red onion quick pickle

Preparation time: 15 mins | Cooking time: 0 mins | Servings: 4

Ingredients

- Hot water, 1 cup (250g)
- Rice vinegar, 1 cup (250g)
- Sugar, 4tbsp (60g)
- Salt, ½ tsp (2.5g)
- Carrots that have been peeled or thinly sliced red onions, 16 oz (480g)
- Finely sliced, fresh ginger that has been peeled, 2 inch

Procedure

1. In a jar with a lid, combine the salt, boiling water, rice vinegar, and sugar. Shake ferociously until the salt and sugar are combined.
2. After placing the carrots and ginger slices in the jar, gently stir the pickling liquid with a spoon. Tighten the cover and let the mixture to come to room temperature before putting the jar in the refrigerator.
3. Try to create these quick pickles a day or two before serving the carrots on board. Put red onions on the Board because the flavor of them will get better the longer they wait.

Nutrition per Serving:

Calories – 149 | Fat - 2g | Carbs - 29g | Protein - 2g | Sugar – 14g | Fiber – 3g | Potassium - 1469mg | Sodium – 148mg | Cholesterol 0mg

7.18 Quinoa and Pitta board

Preparation time: 15 mins |
Cooking time: 0 mins | Servings: 8

Ingredients

- Quinoa Salad, 4 cups (1000g)
- Triangle-shaped pita breads, 6 (90g)
- Thinly sliced cucumber, ½ cup (125g)
- Hummus with Roasted Red Peppers, 2 cups (500g)
- Wheat crackers, 32
- Pumpkin seeds, 2 cups (500g)
- Drained olives, 1 cup (250g)
- Jar of marinated artichokes, 8 ounces, drained, 2. (240g)
- Olives, 2 jar.
- Hastily prepared red onions, 2 cup (500g)
- Bunch of radishes, cut in half, 2
- Dates, cut in half, and 20.
- Dried apricots, 4 cups (1000g)
- Lemon, cut into wedges, 2.
- Cherry tomatoes on the vine, 12 ounces (360g)
- For garnish, use fresh mint leaves.

Procedure

1. Position the medium bowl of quinoa salad adjacent to the board's left centre. Cover the cucumber with the majority of the pita bread.
2. Set the tiny bowl of Roasted Red Pepper Hummus on the board's opposite side. The bowl is covered in wheat crackers.
3. Arrange the artichokes, capers, olives, pomegranate arils, pickled onions, and olives on the board in small bowls. Place the remaining pita bread around the board's edge between the hummus and the
4. Fill in any gaps on the board with the lemon wedges, dried apricots, figs, and radishes Put the cherry tomatoes in a small bowl as a garnish.

Nutrition per Serving:

Calories – 158 | Fat - 4g | Carbs - 35g | Protein - 8g | Sugar – 7g | Fiber – 6g | Potassium - 3181mg | Sodium – 1382mg | Cholesterol – 0mg

7.19 Fruit board

Preparation time: 15 mins |
Cooking time: 0 mins | Servings: 5

Ingredients

- Sliced kiwis, 1 cup (250g)
- Diced mangoes, 1 cup (250g)
- Grapes, (1 cup (250g)
- Cherries, 8 handfuls
- Figs, ½ cup (125g)
- Sliced peaches, ½ cup (125g)
- Sliced apricots, 1 cup (250g)
- Sliced plums, ½ cup (125g)
- Sliced apple, 2 cup (500g)

Procedure

1. Arrange all fruits on a platter.
2. Then spread out on a big dish and softened at room temperature for 20 to 30 minutes. Fruit should be arranged in clusters.

Nutrition per Serving:

Calories – 611 | Fat - 3g | Carbs - 152g | Protein - 4g | Sugar – 105g | Fiber – 15g | Potassium - 1492mg | Sodium – 821mg | Cholesterol – 0mg

7.20 Vegan Dessert

Preparation time: 30mins |
Cooking time: 0 mins | Servings: 8

Ingredients

Non-dairy Cheese

- Vegan cream cheese, 8 ounces (240g)
- Vegan cheesecake weighing 8 ounces, thinly sliced.

Spreads

- Dessert hummus, 9 oz (270g)
- Jellies or jam, 7 oz (210g)
- Peanut butter spread, ½ cup (125g)
- Melting chocolate, ½ cup (125g)

Dry Fruits or Nuts

- Dried nuts (walnuts, pecans, almonds, etc.), 16 oz (480g)
- Fruits, 8 oz (cranberries, pineapple, etc.) (240g)

Fresh Fruit (just pick a few)

- Berries, 8 oz (raspberries, blueberries) (240g)
- Orange and kiwi slices, 1 cup (250g)
- Grapes (red or green), 1 cup (250g)
- Cherries, ½ cup (125g)
- Figs, ½ cup (125g)
- Pomegranate, 1 cup (250g)

Veggie Cookies

- Vegan wafers and biscotti, 12 pieces (72g)
- Veggie cookies, 12 pieces (144g)

Procedure

1. Add everything, including non- dairy cheeses, to your board.
2. Place all spreads on the board in small bowls or platters.
3. Alternately arrange anything else you are adding on the board. Occasionally, you may create designs with vegan meat and secure them in place with toothpicks.
4. Add garnishes like herb sprigs and serve right now or chill until serving time.

Nutrition per Serving:

Calories – 115 | Fat - 8g | Carbs - 11g | Protein - 2g | Sugar – 6g | Fiber – 5g | Potassium - 310mg | Sodium – 114mg | Cholesterol – 0mg

8 SWEET BREADS

8.1 Strawberry Bread

Preparation time: 15 mins |
Cooking time: 50 mins | Servings: 10

Ingredients

- All purpose flour, 1 and ½ cups (375g)
- Baking powder, 1 ad ½ tsp (7.5g)
- Salt, ¼ tsp (1.25g)
- Oil, ½ cup (125g)
- Eggs, 2
- Vanilla extract, 1 tsp (5g)
- Almond extract, ½ tsp (2.5g)
- Buttermilk, ¾ cup (175g)
- Fresh strawberries, 1 and ½ cup (375g)
- Granulated sugar, 1 tbsp (15g)

Procedure

1. With a rack in the center, preheat the oven to 350°F. A 95-loaf pan should be greased and saved.
2. Flour, baking soda, and salt should all be combined in a medium bowl.
3. Whisk the buttermilk, oil, sugar, eggs, vanilla, and almond extract in a different bowl. Add the dry ingredients and blend by whisking.
4. Combine the strawberries and 1 tbsp of flour in a separate bowl. Except for a few for the top, add the strawberries to the batter and incorporate by stirring with a rubber spatula.
5. Smooth the top after pouring the batter into the prepared loaf pan. 1 tbsp of sugar is sprinkled over the batter and 1 tbsp of the reserved strawberries are placed on top. Until a toothpick put into the center of the cake comes out clean, bake for 45 to 55 minutes. To ensure equal browning, rotate the pan halfway during the baking period. After cooling the pan for 15 minutes on a rack, Serve the sweet strawberry bread on a board.

Nutrition per Serving:

Calories – 285kcal | Fat - 13g | Carbs - 40g | Protein - 5g | Sugar – 24g | Fiber – 1.5g | Potassium - 153mg | Sodium – 90mg | Cholesterol – 37mg

8.2 Cinnamon Swirl Orange Bread

Preparation time: 20 mins |
Cooking time: 60 mins | Servings: 12

Ingredients

- Active dry yeast, ¼ oz (1.5g)
- Warm water, ¼ cup (62.5g)
- Granulated sugar, ½ cup (125g)
- Unsalted butter, ¼ cup (62.5g)
- Grated orange zest, 1tbsp (15g)
- Salt, 1 tsp (5g)
- Orange juice, ¾ cup (175g)
- Bread flour, 6 cups
- Beaten egg, 1.
- Granulate sugar, ½ cup (125g)
- Grounded cinnamon, 1 tbsp (15g) for filling

Procedure

1. Take a measuring cup for liquids Warm water with yeast dissolved; all the w mixture to proof for five to ten minutes.
2. Mix milk, sugar, butter, salt, orange zest, and orange juice in a stand mixer, and let cool to lukewarm (105°F–115°F).
3. Scatter flour. Add 2 cups of flour, then beat until smooth. Beat well after adding the yeast and egg. Add the remaining flour little by little until you have a soft dough.
4. 10 minutes of kneading Place the dough in a sizable, oiled bowl. Cover: allow to rise for about 1 1/2 hours or until it has doubled.
5. Halve the dough after deflating it. Cover and rest for ten minutes.
6. Roll each half into a rectangle. Cinnamon and sugar are combined. Spread half of the sugar mixture over each rectangle. Put each with a teaspoon of water, then smooth with a spatula.
7. Seal the edge; use your hands' sides to press down on the loaf's ends to form two thin, sealed pieces. As you place the bread in the pan, fold the strips under it. In a greased pan, place the sealed edge down. Cover and allow to double.

8. Turn on the oven to 350°F toward the end of the rise. Bake for 25 to 30 minutes, or until golden brown and 200°F inside. To avoid over-browning, cover with foil for the last few minutes, if necessary. Cool off.
9. To prepare to frost, put the ingredients in a small bowl. Use a spoon to drizzle icing on cooled loaves while moving the spoon back and forth.

Nutrition per Serving:
Calories – 219kcal | Fat - 3g | Carbs - 43g | Protein - 5g | Sugar – 14g | Fiber – 1g | Potassium - 234mg | Sodium – 151mg | Cholesterol – 15.5mg

8.3 Pumpkin Chocolate chip Bread

Preparation time: 10 mins |
Cooking time: 35 mins | Serving size: 6

Ingredients

- Pumpkin, 15oz (1 can)
- Eggs, 4
- Vegetable oil, 1 cup (250g)
- Water, 2/3 cup (175g)
- Sugar, 3 cups (600g)
- Flour, 3 cups (600g)
- Baking powder, 2 tsp (30g)
- Salt, nutmeg, and grounded cinnamon, 1 tsp each (5g each)
- Ginger garlic paste, ½ tsp (2.5g)
- Mini chocolate chips, 1 cup (250g)

Procedure

1. The oven to 350 degrees.
2. Grease eight small loaf tins.
3. Mix the pumpkin, eggs, oil, water, and sugar in a sizable basin.
4. Mix the flour, baking soda, salt, cinnamon, nutmeg, cloves, and ginger in a medium bowl.
5. Blend the flour combination thoroughly before adding it to the pumpkin mixture.
6. Add the chocolate chunks and stir.
7. Pour the batter into the little loaf pans in an even layer.
8. When a toothpick placed into the center of the cake comes out clean, bake for 35 to 40 minutes.

Nutrition per Serving:
Calories – 222kcal | Fat - 8g | Carbs - 34g | Protein - 3g | Sugar – 22g | Fiber – 1.5g | Potassium - 180mg | Sodium – 141mg | Cholesterol – 23mg

8.4 Coconut Flour Mini Cheese Loaves

Preparation time: 10 mins |
Cooking time: 15 mins | Servings: 12

Ingredients

- Soft butter, 1 stick (113g)
- Baking powder, 1 tsp (5g)
- Coconut flour, ½ cup (50g)
- Salt and pepper to taste.
- A pinch of chili powder
- Eggs, 8
- Spring onion, ½
- Shredded cheese, 1 cup (100g)
- Sliced pepperoni stick, 1 for topping.
- Pumpkin seeds, 2 tbsp (30g)

Procedure

1. Blend the softened butter, baking powder, salt, pepper, optional red pepper flakes, and coconut flour until smooth.
2. One by one, add the eggs. After adding each egg, stir.
3. Sliced spring onions and grated or shredded cheese should be gently incorporated (reserve some to top each loaf).
4. Assemble each tiny loaf pan (or muffin cases).
5. My preferred toppings for mini loaves are a couple of pieces of pepperoni, some grated or shredded cheese, and a few pumpkin seeds.
6. Bake for 15 minutes, or until brown, at 180C/350F.

Nutrition per Serving:

Calories – 161kcal | Fat - 10g | Carbs - 14g | Protein - 6.5g | Sugar – 0.5g | Fiber – 2.2g | Potassium - 86mg | Sodium – 169mg | Cholesterol – 62mg

8.5 Quick Cheese Bread

Preparation time: 15 mins |
Cooking time: 60 mins | Servings: 12

Ingredients

- Flour, 2 cups (200g)
- Baking powder, 4tsp (20g)
- Salt, ½ tsp (2g)
- Cold butter, ¼ cup (62g)
- Cayenne pepper, 1/8 tsp (1g)
- Shredded cheddar, 1 cup (100g)
- Parmesan cheese, 2tbsp (30g)
- Green onion, 1
- Eggs, 2
- Milk, 1 cup (100g)
- Sugar, 3 tbsp (45g)

Procedure

1. Set the oven to 350°F. Griddle an 8" x 4" loaf pan.
2. In a medium bowl, whisk the dry ingredients.
3. Cut in butter using a fork or a pastry cutter. Cheese and green onions are stirred in.
4. Whisk eggs in another basin until frothy. Add sugar and milk.
5. Do not overmix; simply combine the dry ingredients with the wet ones.
6. Fill the prepared pan with the mixture, and bake for 50 minutes, or until the toothpick comes out clean.

Nutrition per Serving:

Calories – 184 | Fat - 8g | Carbs - 22g | Protein - 6g | Sugar – 5g | Fiber – 1g | Potassium - 206mg | Sodium – 224mg | Cholesterol – 31mg

8.6 Chocolate Chip Red Velvet Bread

Preparation time: 15 mins |
Cooking time: 40 mins | Servings: 9

Ingredients

- Bittersweet Chocolate, 6oz (180g)
- Water, ½ cup (125g)
- Brown sugar, (300g)
- Soft butter, ½ cup (50g)
- Eggs, 6
- Vanilla extract, 3tsp (15g)
- Sour cream, 1 and ½ cup (150g)
- Red food color, 3 tbsp (45g)
- All-purpose flour, 4 cups (400g)
- Baking soda, 3 tsp (15g)
- Salt, 1 and ½ tsp (7.5g)
- Mini Chocolate chips, 1 cup (!00g)

For Icing

- Confectioners sugar, 3 cups (300g)
- Milk, 3tbsp (15g)
- Snowflakes sprinkles

Procedure

1. Set the oven's temperature to 350°F (180°C).
2. 3 small loaf pans should only have the bottoms coated with baking spray.
3. Bittersweet chocolate and water should be combined in a small saucepan.
4. Set the oven's temperature to 350.
5. 3 small loaf pans should only have the bottoms coated with baking spray.
6. Bittersweet chocolate and water should be combined in a small saucepan.
7. Stirring occasionally, heat on low heat until the chocolate melts.
8. The food should be taken off the heat and left to cool to room temperature.
9. Combine the brown sugar, butter, eggs, and vanilla in a sizable basin.
10. until creamy, whisk well.
11. Add the sour cream and the mixture of melted chocolate. Once more whisk until smooth.
12. Add the small chocolate chips by blending.
13. Fill the loaf pans with the prepared batter.
14. The toothpick test should come out clean after 35 to 40 minutes of baking.
15. On a cooling rack, the loaves are cooled in their pans.
16. Remove once it has cooled, then make the frosting.
17. Use a fork to stir 1 tablespoon of milk at a time into the confectioner's sugar in a bowl until the appropriate consistency is reached.
18. Sprinkle snowflake sprinkles on top of the icing before drizzling it over the cake loaves. Enjoy or package up and give as gifts to family and friends.

Nutrition per Serving:

Calories – 1206kcal | Fat - 56g | Carbs - 189g | Protein - 14g | Sugar – 134g | Fiber – 2g | Potassium - 346mg | Sodium – 812mg | Cholesterol – 125mg

8.7 Brown Sugar Banana Bread

Preparation time: 20 mins |
Cooking time: 45 mins | Servings: 12

Ingredients

- Butter, ½ cup (125g) (g)
- Brown sugar, 1 cup (200g)
- Eggs, 2
- Bananas, 6
- Vanilla extract, 1 tsp (5g)
- Ground cinnamon, 1 tsp (5g)
- Flour, 2 cups (250g)
- Baking powder and baking soda, 1 tsp each (5g)
- A pinch of salt

Procedure

1. Grease and line a normal loaf pan with baking paper as the oven is preheated to 350°F (180°C).
2. Butter and sugar should be combined in a mixing dish until light and fluffy. Add the eggs one at a time, beating well after each addition.
3. Mix thoroughly after adding the vanilla essence and bananas.
4. The dry ingredients should be combined and then stirred into the batter.
5. Place the batter in the loaf pan that has been prepared.
6. Sprinkle the banana bread with the sugar and cinnamon mixture that has been combined for the topping.
7. Bake the tin for 45 minutes, or until a skewer inserted into the center comes out clean.
8. Before serving, take the food out of the oven and let it cool.

Nutrition per Serving:

Calories – 228 | Fat - 7g | Carbs - 38g | Protein - 5g | Sugar – 19g | Fiber – 2g | Potassium - 100mg | Sodium – 20mg | Cholesterol – 32mg

8.8 Strawberry Banana Bread

Preparation time: 10 mins |
Cooking time: 1 hour 5 mins | Servings: 10

Ingredients

- All purpose flour, 2 and ½ cups (250g)
- Sugar and vanilla yogurt, ¾ cup each (175g)
- Unsalted butter, 4 tbsp (60g)
- Salt, ½ tsp (2g)
- Beaten eggs, 2.
- Ripe Bananas, 3
- Vanilla extract, 2 tsp (10g)
- Diced strawberries, 1 cup (100g)

Procedure

1. Reheat your oven to 350°F (180°C).and spray cooking spray in a 9 by 5-inch bread pan.
2. Mix the flour, baking soda, and salt in a medium bowl.
3. Butter and sugar are whisked together in a sizable bowl. The yogurt, eggs, bananas, and vanilla are then whisked in.
4. Fold the liquid components and flour mixture together gently until just mixed. Don't overmix, please.
5. Add the strawberries and stir slowly. It will be a very thick batter.
6. Add the strawberries and stir slowly. It will be a very thick batter.
7. A toothpick inserted in the center of the bread should come out clean or with a few crumbs after 60 to 65 minutes of baking (it took 63 minutes).
8. Allow the bread to cool in the pan for ten minutes. Before slicing, take out and place on a cooling rack for an hour.
9. This dish won't keep as long as typical banana bread because it contains fresh strawberries. This should be consumed within two to three days and kept in an airtight, transparent container.

Nutrition per Serving:

Calories – 271 | Fat - 7g | Carbs - 51g | Protein - 4g | Sugar – 22g | Fiber – 3g | Potassium - 173mg | Sodium – 231mg | Cholesterol – 38mg

8.9 Apple Streusel Bread

Preparation time: 15 mins |
Cooking time: 50 mins | Servings: 10

Ingredients

- Butter, ½ cup (50g)
- Granulated sugar, 1 cup (100g)
- Eggs, 2
- Milk, ½ cup
- Vanilla extract, 1 tbsp (15g)
- All-purpose flour, 2 cups (200g)
- Salt, ½ tsp (2.5g)
- Baking soda, 1 tsp (5g)
- Cinnamon, 1 tbsp (15g)
- Apples, 1 and ½ cups (150g)

Streusel Topping

- Cold Butter, 5 tbsp (75g)
- White and brown sugar, 2 tbsp each (30g)
- Flour, 1/3 cup (75g)
- Cinnamon, 2 tsp (10g)

Procedure

1. The oven should be preheated to 350°F (180°C). Spray nonstick and use parchment paper to line a loaf pan. Place aside.
2. Butter and sugar are combined in a mixing basin. Stir in the milk, vanilla, and eggs. Mix in the baking soda, salt, flour, and cinnamon until thoroughly blended. Add apple pieces and fold. Fill the prepared loaf pan with the batter. Place aside.
3. Streusel components should be combined in a separate dish and mashed together with a fork to create a crumbly, sand-like texture. Pour mixture into loaf pan containing apple bread batter.
4. When a toothpick is placed into the center of the bread, it should come out clean after 50 to 55 minutes of baking. Set apart for cooling. Make the glaze, then drizzle it over the bread. Serve and savor.

Nutrition per Serving:

Calories – 384 | Fat - 16g | Carbs - 55g | Protein - 6g | Sugar – 31g | Fiber – 1.5g | Potassium - 96mg | Sodium – 378mg | Cholesterol – 37mg

8.10 Starbucks Lemon Bread

Preparation time: 10 mins |
Cooking time: 50 mins | Servings: 10

Ingredients

- Eggs, 3
- Granulated sugar and sour cream, 1 cup each.
- Canoa/Vegetable oil, ½ cup (50g)
- Lemon zest, 2 tbsp (30g)
- Lemon extract, 2 tbsp (30g)
- All purpose flour, 1 and ½ cups (150g)
- Baking powder, 2 tsp (10g)
- Salt to taste

Lemon Glaze

- Confectioners' sugar, 1 cup (100g)
- Lemon juice, 3tbsp

Procedure

1. Oven is heated to 350°F (180°C).
2. Produce the Loaf.
3. The eggs, sugar, and sour cream should all be added to a large bowl and whisked well to mix. While whisking to blend, drizzle in the oil.
4. Whisk in the lemon extract and zest after adding them.
5. Don't overmix; add the flour, baking powder, and salt and stir just until incorporated.
6. Turn the batter into the pan that has been prepared, lightly smoothing the top with a spatula.
7. A toothpick inserted in the middle crack should come out clean, and the top should be domed and set after 50 to 52 minutes of baking. To avoid the bread's top and edges from excessive browning before the middle is cooked through, cover the pan with foil during the final 10 minutes of baking.
8. The loaf cools in the pan on top of a wire rack for at least 30 minutes.
9. Before slicing and serving, spread the glaze over the bread in an even layer.

Nutrition per Serving:

Calories – 329 | Fat - 20g | Carbs - 49g | Protein - 7g | Sugar – 32g | Fiber – 0.5g | Potassium - 325mg | Sodium – 233mg | Cholesterol – 56mg

8.11 Homemade Cherry Bread

Preparation time: 20 mins |
Cooking time: 50 mins | Servings: 10

Ingredients

- All-purpose Flour, 2 and ½ cups (250g)
- Granulated sugar, 1 and ¼ cups (125g)
- Baking powder, 1 and ½ tsp (7.5g)
- A pinch of salt
- Butter, 1 cup (100g)
- Milk, ¾ cup (75g)
- Eggs, 2
- Vanilla, 1 tsp (5g)
- Cherries, 1-2 cups (100-200g)

Procedure

1. Turn on the oven to 375°F (190C).
2. The flour, sugar, baking powder, and salt should be combined in a large bowl before adding the butter and combining to produce a crumbly mixture. To make your crumb topping, take 3/4 cup of the mixture and set it aside.
3. Whisk or use a fork to combine the milk, eggs, and vanilla in a medium bowl. With a wooden spoon or spatula, add it to the flour mixture and stir just until incorporated. There should be some lumps in the batter. Avoid overmixing.
4. Add the cherries after folding, then spoon the mixture into the loaf pan. Add some crumb topping on top. Bake for around 50 to 60 minutes. Use a toothpick to test the doneness. Before serving, let cool entirely on a wire rack when it has finished cooling in the loaf pan. Enjoy!

Nutrition per Serving:

Calories – 407 | Fat - 21g | Carbs - 6g | Protein - 53g | Sugar – 29g | Fiber – 1.2g | Potassium - 115mg | Sodium – 306mg | Cholesterol – 35mg

8.12 Pine Apple Bread

Preparation time: 15 min |
Cooking time: 55 min | Servings: 8

Ingredients

- Sugar, ¾ cup (75g)
- Soft unsalted butter, ½ cup (50g)
- Eggs, 2
- All-purpose flour, 1 and ½ cups (150)
- Baking powder, 2 tsp (!0g)
- Whole milk, 2tbsp (30g)
- Crushed pineapple, 1 cup (100g)
- Pineapple Syrup, ¼ cup (25g)
- Salt to taste

Glaze

- Powdered Sugar, 1 cup (100g)
- Vanilla extract, 1 tsp (5g)
- Pineapple syrup, 2 tbsp (30g)

Procedure

1. Set the oven to 350°F (180°C). A pan should be greased, nonstick spray-coated, or lined with parchment paper.
2. Butter and sugar should be whisked together in a sizable bowl until light and fluffy. Add each of the two eggs one at a time.
3. Salt, baking powder, and flour should all be combined. Then combine the egg mixture with the pineapple syrup and half of the dry ingredients. Mix gently, then add the remaining flour and milk and stir again. The crushed pineapple is then added and mixed.
4. Pour the mixture into the prepared pan and bake for 45–55 minutes on the middle rack. When a toothpick put in the center of the bread comes out clean, the bread is ready. Tent the top with aluminum foil if it starts to brown too much. After about 10 minutes, remove the bread and let it cool.
5. To prepare the glaze, combine powdered sugar, vanilla, and pineapple syrup in a bowl. Next, evenly distribute it over the bread.

Nutrition per Serving:

Calories – 356kcal | Fat - 14g | Carbs - 59g | Protein - 5g | Sugar – 39g | Fiber – 2.3g | Potassium - 190mg | Sodium – 58mg | Cholesterol – 42mg

8.13 Chocolate Chip Peanut Butter Bread

Preparation time: 15 mins |
Cooking time: 50 mins | Servings: 10

Ingredients

- All purpose flour, 1 and ¾ cups (175g)
- Baking soda and salt, ½ tsp each (2.5g)
- Baking powder, 1 tsp (5g)
- Creamy Peanut butter, ¾ cup (75g)
- Brown sugar, ½ cup (50g)
- Vegetable oil, ¼ cup (25g)
- Egg, 1 ; Vanilla extract, 1 tsp (5g)
- Buttermilk, ¾ cup (75g)
- Dark Chocolate chips, 1 & 1/3 cups (125g)

Procedure

1. Set the oven to 350°F (180°C). A 9x5 loaf pan should be lightly greased and lined with parchment paper.
2. Salt, baking soda, baking powder, and flour should be combined and sifted.
3. In a mixing bowl, combine the peanut butter, sugar, oil, egg, and vanilla. Make sure to beat thoroughly to ensure even mixing.
4. Beginning and ending with the dry ingredients, add the half and a half to the bowl in alternating motions. Add a cup of chocolate chips and combine.
5. Spread the batter into the pan that has been prepared, then smooth the top. At this point, the batter will appear a little greasy. Add the remaining 1/3 cup of chips on top, then bake the bread for 50–55 minutes.
6. After allowing the bread to cool in the pan for five minutes, carefully transfer it to a rack. Attempt to wait a little while longer to slice the bread because it tastes so good and warm.

Nutrition per Serving:

Calories – 311kcal | Fat - 8.5g | Carbs - 28g | Protein - 7g | Sugar – 8g | Fiber – 2g | Potassium - 180mg | Sodium – 269mg | Cholesterol – 18.5mg

8.14 Almond Coconut Bread

Preparation time: 20 mins |
Cooking time: 50 mins | Servings: 12

Ingredients

- Almond flour, 1 and ½ cups (35g)
- Coconut flour, 2 tbsp (30g)
- Golden flax seeds, ¼ cup (25g)
- Psyllium husk powder, 1 and ½ tsp (4g)
- Salt to taste
- Brown sugar, 1 cup (100g)
- Baking soda, 1 tsp (4.6g)
- Baking powder, ½ tsp (2.3g)
- Egg, 5
- Coconut oil, ¼ cup (25g)
- Apple cider vinegar, 1 tbsp (15g)
- Pumpkin seeds, 2 tbsp (30g)

Procedure

1. Set the oven to 350°F (180°C).
2. Baking paper should be lined with cooking spray.
3. To combine and make sure the flour is fine, add the dry ingredients to a food processor and pulse a few times.
4. The eggs, coconut oil, honey, and apple cider vinegar are lightly beaten in another bowl.
5. Pulse the addition with the dry components until the batter is combined.
6. Two-thirds of the seeds should be added to the batter after removing the blender's blade.
7. Pour the batter into the loaf pan that has been preheated, then top with the remaining seeds.
8. A skewer should come out clean after 45 to 50 minutes of baking on the bottom shelf.
9. Check the bread after 20 to 25 minutes and cover it with parchment paper if it appears to be getting too black while baking.

Nutrition per Serving:

Calories – 169kcal | Fat - 14g | Carbs - 40g | Protein - 6g | Sugar – 5g | Fiber – 4.2g | Potassium - 91mg | Sodium – 253mg | Cholesterol – 0mg

8.15 Oatmeal Quick Bread

Preparation time: 10 mins |
Cooking time: 40 mins | Servings: 3

Ingredients

- All-purpose flour, 1 and 1/3 cups (g)
- Old fashioned quick oats, 2/3 cups (75g)
- Granulated white sugar, 1/3 cup (20g)
- Brown sugar, 1/3 cup (20g)
- Baking powder, 1 and ½ tsp (7.5g)
- Baking soda, ¾ tsp (75g)
- Cinnamon and salt, ½ tsp each (2.5g)
- Chocolate chips, 1/3 cup (20g)
- Egg, 1
- Buttermilk, 1 cup (!00g)
- Melted butter, 3 tbsp (45g)

Procedure

1. Set the oven's temperature to 350°F (180°C). A 95 loaf pan should be greased and saved.
2. Mix the flour, oats, sugar, brown sugar, baking soda, cinnamon, salt, and chocolate chips in a sizable basin.
3. Combine the buttermilk, egg, and melted butter in a small bowl.
4. Just until thoroughly mixed, add the wet mixture to the dry mixture and whisk with a wooden spoon or rubber spatula. It will be lumpy batter.
5. When the loaf pan is ready, pour the batter into it. Bake the loaf for 40 to 45 minutes, or until a toothpick inserted in the center comes out clean.
6. Before slicing to serve, allow it to cool on a rack.

Nutrition per Serving:

Calories – 195kcal | Fat - 6g | Carbs - 80g | Protein - 9g | Sugar – 18g | Fiber – 3.1g | Potassium - 141mg | Sodium – 279mg | Cholesterol – 18.5mg

8.16 Chocolate Zucchini Bread

Preparation time: 10 mins |
Cooking time: 70 mins | Servings: 6

Ingredients

- Grated Zucchini, 4 cups (400g)
- All-purpose flour, 2 and ½ cups (250g)
- Sweetened Cocoa, ½ cup (50g)
- Baking soda, 2 tsp (10g)
- Salt, ½ tsp (2.5g)
- Cinnamon, 1 tsp (5g)
- Sugar, 1 and ½ cup (150g)
- Eggs, 2
- Unsalted butter, ¾ cup (75g)
- Instant coffee granules, ½ tsp (2.5g)

Procedure

1. With a rack in the center, preheat the oven to 350°F (180°C). Two 9x5-inch loaf pans should be greased with butter or baking spray.
2. In a sizable basin, thoroughly combine the flour, unsweetened cocoa, baking soda, salt, and cinnamon. Mix the items together and whisk until there are no more clumps.
3. The sugar and eggs should be combined in a different, big bowl and beaten for about a minute. This can be done either manually with a wooden spoon or with an electric mixer set to medium speed. (I use a mixer because I'm lazy but doing it by hand is doable.
4. Beat till smooth after including the melted butter, instant coffee granules, and almond essence.
5. Combine the sugar and egg mixture with the chopped zucchini. 3 times, stirring after each addition, add the flour to the zucchini mixture.
6. Divide the batter between the two prepared loaf pans. Put inside the oven for 50 minutes of baking at 350°F.
7. After allowing the bread to cool and then allow the food to cool fully on a rack.

Nutrition per Serving:

Calories: 197 | Fat: 8g | Carbohydrates - 29g | Protein: 4g | Sugar: 16g | Fiber – 2g | Potassium: 215mg | Sodium: 188mg | Cholesterol – 25mg

8.17 Filipino Spanish Bread with Sweet Buttery Filling

Preparation time: 60 mins |
Cooking time: 20 mins | Servings: 5

Ingredients

- All-purpose flour, 3 cups (300g)
- Instant yeast, 1 ad ½ tsp (7.5g)
- White sugar, ¼ cup (25g)
- Salt, 1 tsp (5g)
- Milk, ¾ cup (75g)
- Butter, ½ cup (50g)
- Egg, 1
- Breadcrumbs, ½ cup (50g)
- Flour, 2 tsp (10g)
- Brown sugar, ½ cup (50g)

Procedure

1. Mix flour, sugar, salt, egg, lukewarm milk, melted butter, and yeast to form a slightly sticky dough.
2. Knead on an oiled surface until smooth, then let rise in a warm spot until doubled.
3. For the filling, cook butter, breadcrumbs, milk or water, sugar, and salt until thick, stirring into a paste.
4. Punch down risen dough, divide into 16 pieces, and wrap each around the filling. Bake for 20 minutes at 150°C (300°F).
5. Enjoy the Spanish bread warm from the oven.

Nutrition per Serving:

Calories: 211 | Fat: 6g | Carbohydrates: 34g | Protein: 5g | Sugar: 11g | Fiber – 1g | Potassium: 80mg | Sodium: 268mg | Cholesterol – 20mg

8.18 Peach Cobbler Bread

Preparation time: 15 mins |
Cooking time: 50 mins | Servings: 8

Ingredients

- Butter, 1/3 cup (20g)
- Sugar, 1 cup (100g)
- Eggs, 2
- Water, 1/3 cup (20g)
- Vanilla extract, 1tsp (5g)
- Almond extract, 1/8 tsp
- Diced peaches, 1 cup (100g)
- All-purpose flour, 1 and ½ cups (150g)
- Baking soda, 1 tsp (5g)
- Baking powder, ¼ tsp (1g)
- Chopped pecans, ½ cup (50g)
- Brown sugar, 2 tbsp (30g)
- Chopped pecans, 2 tbsp (30g) for topping.

Procedure

1. Cream the butter and sugar in a bowl. One at a time, add the eggs, beating thoroughly after each addition. Add water and extracts by beating. Add peaches and stir. Add the flour, baking powder, salt, and baking soda to the creamed mixture gradually. Add pecans and stir.
2. Fill a 9x5-inch loaf pan with the mixture. Sprinkle topping over batter after combining the ingredients. A toothpick inserted in the center of the cake should come out clean after 50 to 55 minutes of baking at 350°. Before removing from pan to a wire rack, let cool for 10 minutes.

Nutrition per Serving:

Calories: 182 | Fat: 8g | Carbohydrates: 26g | Protein: 3g | Sugar: 15g | Fiber – 2.5g | Potassium: 286mg | Sodium: 206mg | Cholesterol – 25mg

8.19 Sweet Potato Bread

Preparation time: 15 mins |
Cooking time: 60 mins | Servings: 12

Ingredients

- White sugar, 1 and ½ cups (150g)
- Vegetable oil, ½ cup (50g)
- Eggs, 2
- All-purpose flour, 1 and ½ cups (150g)
- Baking soda, 1 tsp (5g)
- Grounded cinnamon and nutmeg, ½ tsp each (2.5g each)
- Salt to taste
- Water, 1/3 cup (20g)
- Cooked and mashed sweet potato, 1 cup (100g)
- Chopped pecans, ½ cup (50g)

Procedure

1. Set the oven to 350°F (180°C). Butter a 9x5-inch loaf pan.
2. Beat sugar and oil together in a big bowl. Add the eggs and mix thoroughly. In another basin, mix the flour, baking soda, cinnamon, nutmeg, and salt. Alternately stir water and the flour mixture into the egg mixture. Add the chopped nuts and the sweet potatoes. Fill the prepared loaf pan with the batter.
3. Bake in the preheated oven for approximately an hour, or until a toothpick inserted in the center comes out clean.

Nutrition per Serving:

Calories: 303 | Fat: 15g | Carbohydrates: 46g | Protein: 5g | Sugar: 26g | Fiber – 3g | Potassium: 131mg | Sodium: 171mg | Cholesterol – 15mg

8.20 Carrot Cake Bread

Servings: 9 | Preparation time: 20 mins |
Cooking time: 55 mins

Ingredients

- All-purpose flour, 1 and 1/3 cups (120g)
- Ground ginger, ½ tsp (2.5g)
- Nutmeg, ¼ tsp (1g)
- Salt to taste
- Baking powder, 2 and ½ tsp (12.5g)
- Eggs, 2
- Granulated sugar, ½ cup (50g)
- Vegetable oil, ½ cup (50g)
- Vanilla extract, 1 tsp (5g)
- Grated Carrots 2 cups (200g)
- Chopped pecans, ½ cup (50g)

For Glaze

- Cream cheese, 4 oz (120g)
- Unsalted butter, 4 tbsp (60g)
- Powdered sugar, 1 and ½ cup (150g)
- Vanilla extract, ¼ tsp
- A pinch of salt

Procedure

1. Preheat the oven to 350°F (180°C) and line a loaf pan with parchment paper with an overhang for easy removal. In a medium bowl, whisk together flour, salt, nutmeg, ginger, cinnamon, and baking powder. In a large bowl, lightly mix eggs, sugars, oil, and vanilla. Stir in pecans and carrots briefly, then combine with dry ingredients. Pour batter into the pan, baking for 50-55 minutes until a toothpick comes out clean. Cool before icing. For the glaze, beat cream cheese, butter, salt, vanilla, and powdered sugar until smooth. Microwave for 20 seconds to soften before drizzling on cooled bread.

Nutrition per Serving:

Calories: 367 | Fat: 16g | Carbohydrates: 54g | Protein: 4g | Sugar: 39g | Fiber – 3.5g | Potassium: 290mg | Sodium: 146mg | Cholesterol – 30mg

9 SAUCES, CONDIMENTS, DIPS FOR CHARCUTERIE BOARDS

9.1 Classic Charcuterie sauce

Preparation time: 5 mins |
Cooking time: 25 mins | Servings: 8

Ingredients

- Demi-glace, 3 tbsp (45g)
- Chopped onions, ½ cup (125g)
- Unsalted butter, 2 teaspoons (10g)
- White wine, 1 cup (250g)
- Dried mustard, 2 tbsp (30g)
- Lemon juice, 1 tsp (5g)
- Sugar, ½ tsp (2.5g)
- Finely chopped cornichons for decoration, ½ cup (125g)

Procedure

1. Assemble the components.
2. Lemon juice and sugar should be combined in a small bowl; whisk until sugar is dissolved.
3. Melt butter and sauté onions in it until they are tender and transparent.
4. Wine should be added, the mixture should be heated until it boils, then the heat should be dropped slightly so that it simmers for another two minutes.
5. Demi-glace should be added after which the heat should be reduced to a simmer for ten minutes.
6. Pass through a mesh strainer to filter. Add the sugar-lemon combination and mustard.
7. Serve immediately after adding chopped cornichons as a garnish.

Nutrition per Serving:

Calories – 177 | Fat - 10g | Carbs - 11g | Protein - 7g | Sugar – 4g | Fiber – 1.5g | Potassium - 651mg | Sodium – 644mg | Cholesterol – 15mg

9.2 Dijion mustard sauce

Preparation time: 5 mins |
Cooking time: 25 mins | Servings: 4

Ingredients

- Minced shallot, 1 oz (30g)
- Split butter, 2 oz (60g)
- White wine, 2 ounces (60g)
- Demi-glace, 1 cup (250g)
- Dijon mustard, 1 tbsp (15g)
- Cornichons, 4 diced 1 oz (30g)
- Lemon juice, fresh, ½ tsp (2.5g)
- Pepper and salt to taste.

Procedure

1. The shallot should be sauteed in butter until transparent.
2. When it has thickened to a syrupy consistency, add the white wine.
3. Add the demi-glace, whisk, and reduce the sauce until it coats the back of a spoon.
4. Include the mustard, cornichons, and lemon juice.
5. While whisking, add the final ounce of butter.
6. Add pepper and salt as per taste.

Nutrition per Serving:

Calories – 180 | Fat - 7g | Carbs - 4g | Protein - 2g | Sugar – 0g | Fiber – 0.5g | Potassium - 69mg | Sodium – 129mg | Cholesterol – 20mg

9.3 Garlic aioli dip

Preparation time: 5 mins |
Cooking time: 5 mins | Servings: 10

Ingredients

- Mayonnaise, ¾ cup (187g)
- Minced garlic cloves, 4 pieces
- Lemon juice, 2 ½ tsp (12.5g)
- Salt, ¾ tsp (3.75g)
- Black pepper, grounded, ½ tsp (2.5g)

Procedure

1. Take a bowl and mix lemon juice, garlic, mayonnaise, salt, and pepper together.
2. Before serving, cover and chill for at least 30 minutes.

Nutrition per Serving:

Calories – 151 | Fat - 16g | Carbs - 2g | Protein - 0g | Sugar – 0g | Fiber – 0.2g | Potassium - 15mg | Sodium – 336mg | Cholesterol – 8mg

9.4 Mushroom Sauce

Preparation time: 5 mins |
Cooking time: 20 mins | Servings: 4

Ingredients

- Butter, 1 oz (30g)
- Mushrooms, 0.5 pounds (226g)
- Finely chopped onion, 0.25 cup (62g)
- Dried tarragon, 1 tsp (5g)
- White wine, 0.5 cup (125g)
- Veal stock, 1 cup (250g)
- Full-fat cream, 0.25 cup (62g)
- Blanched, julienne-cut, and cut gherkins, 0.25 cup (62g)
- Dijon mustard, 1 tbsp (15g)

Procedure

1. Sauté onions in butter on low heat. Add mushrooms and tarragon, sautéing on high until browned. Pour in stock and white wine, simmer for 5 minutes. Stir in cream and reduce until sauce thickens to coat a spoon.

Nutrition per Serving:

Calories – 180 | Fat - 4g | Carbs - 16g | Protein - 3g | Sugar – 0g | Fiber – 2g | Potassium - 402mg | Sodium – 133mg | Cholesterol – 12mg

9.5 Simple kale and cashew pesto (vegan)

Preparation time: 10 mins |
Cooking time: 0 mins | Servings: 10

Ingredients

- Fresh kale, cleaned and torn, 3 cups (750g)
- Uncooked cashews, ½ cup (125g)
- Garlic cloves, depending on flavor, 2.
- Olive oil, 1 ¼ cup (312g)
- Lemon juice, 2 tbsp. (30g)
- Lemon, 1
- Nutritional yeast, 1tbsp (15g)
- Sea salt, as per taste

Procedure

1. Garlic, cashews, and kale should all be added to a food processor and pulsed until minced finely.
2. Once more pulse until mixed after adding the lemon zest, lemon juice, olive oil and nutritional yeast.
3. To your taste, add extra salt or lemon.
4. Serve straight away or store in an airtight container for up to a week.

Nutrition per Serving:

Calories – 73 | Fat - 0g | Carbs - 4g | Protein - 2g | Sugar – 0g | Fiber – 1.8g | Potassium - 156mg | Sodium – 8mg | Cholesterol – 0mg

9.6 Jam made in a small batch with strawberry sangria

Preparation time: 2h |
Cooking time: 20 mins | Servings: 8

Ingredients

- Freshly cut, quartered, and rinsed strawberries, 2 pounds (907g)
- Depending on how sweet the berries are, use 1 cup of sugar. (250g)
- Any preferred wine, red or white, ½ cup (125g)
- Peach liqueur, 1tbsp (15g)
- Orange, 1 cup (250g)
- Lemon, 1
- Orange juice, 1 cup (250g)

Procedure

1. To a sizable mixing bowl, combine every ingredient from the list and Stir.
2. To enable the flavors to meld, keep at room temperature for at least two and maybe up to four hours. Alternately, you could cover the bowl and keep it in the fridge all night.
3. Take a large size saucepan and add strawberry over medium heat and frequently stir. Mash the berries to the desired consistency as they soften.
4. Juice should be tasted and adjusted as needed. Add additional sugar if it doesn't have enough sweetness. Add more lemon juice if it is overly sweet.
5. Cook for 15-20 minutes, or until the jam thickens, after bringing to a boil.
6. Pour the mixture into clean jars, cover them, and keep them in the fridge for up to a month.
7. Cook's note: The only pectin used in this jam is the fruit's natural pectin. As a result, the jam doesn't generate a solid texture like jelly and instead stays soft. Add pectin and follow the instructions on the package for a firmer texture.

Nutrition per Serving:

Calories – 508 | Fat - 2g | Carbs - 114g | Protein - 3g | Sugar – 100g | Fiber – 4g | Potassium - 774mg | Sodium – 8mg | Cholesterol – 0mg

9.7 Blueberry jam with jalapeno

Preparation time: 5 mins |
Cooking time: 20 mins | Servings: 8

Ingredients

- Water, 1 cup (250g)
- Mashed blueberries, 4 cups (1000g)
- Sugar, 3 cups (750g)
- Lemon juice, 1 tbsp (15g)
- Pectin, 1 packet.
- Jalapeño peppers, diced small, 2.

Procedure

1. Wash the blueberries, then cut off the stems.
2. A big pot should be filled with water, blueberries, sugar, and lemon juice. Bring to a simmer. Break up blueberries.
3. Adding peppers and pectin after bringing to a boil.
4. Cook pectin as directed on the packet.
5. Sterilize the jars before canning. Jars must be stored in the refrigerator if they aren't sterilized.
6. Remove from the heat, then pour into jar, and carefully seal.

Nutrition per Serving:

Calories – 210 | Fat - 2g | Carbs - 3g | Protein - 3g | Sugar – 0g | Fiber – 1.2g | Potassium - 640mg | Sodium – 320mg | Cholesterol – 0mg

9.8 Salsa roasted with pepper.

Preparation time: 10 mins |
Cooking time: 10 mins | Servings: 8

Ingredients

- Sweet Baby Peppers, 1 lb. (453g)
- Jalapeno, 1
- Red wine vinegar, 1/4 cup (62g)
- Juice of lemons, two tbsp.(30g)
- Sea salt, ¾ tsp (3g)
- Black pepper, ¼ tsp (1.2g)

Procedure

1. Heat the broiler. Jalapeno and peppers on a sheet pan, broil until blistered on the top oven rack (five minutes).
2. After three minutes of broiling, flip. The peppers should cool.
3. Take out the seeds and stems. Red wine vinegar, sea salt, ¼ of a Jalapeno, pepper, and lemon juice are added to a food processor to emulsify the peppers. Add onions and stir.

Nutrition per Serving:

Calories – 27 | Fat - 1g | Carbs - 6g | Protein - 1g | Sugar – 3g | Fiber – 1.5g | Potassium - 165mg | Sodium – 149mg | Cholesterol – 0mg

9.9 Roasted red pepper sauce for vegans.

Preparation time: 5 mins |
Cooking time: 35 mins | Servings: 10

Ingredients

- Minced garlic, 4 cloves
- Onion chopped, ½ cup (125g)
- Red pepper flakes, pinch
- Chopped and dried roasted red peppers, 4 ½ cup (125g)
- Fire-roasted tomato, 2 28oz cans (840g)
- Chopped fresh parsley with no stems, ¼ cup (62g)
- Fresh basil chopped, 1tbsp (15g)
- Fresh oregano chopped, 1 tbsp (15g)

Procedure

1. In a big pot of soup, heat some oil. Add sea salt and onions, till transparent, sauté.
2. Include the garlic and the chili flakes. For one minute, cook. Add tomatoes and roasted red peppers. To bring the sauce to a simmer, turn up the heat to high.
3. After boiling, lower the heat to medium and boil the sauce for 30 minutes with a half cover.
4. Put the herb-infused sauce in the food processor. Blend until you get the consistency you want. Replacing it in the pot will reheat it. Enjoy!

Nutrition per Serving:

Calories – 10 | Fat - 1g | Carbs - 2g | Protein - 1g | Sugar – 1g | Fiber – 0.8g | Potassium - 51mg | Sodium – 320mg | Cholesterol – 0mg

9.10 Raspberry fig chia jam

Preparation time: 10 mins |
Cooking time: 0 mins | Servings: 2

Ingredients

- Big green frozen figs (defrosted), 3 oz (90g)
- Strawberry, 1 large cup (250g)
- Chia seeds, 1 tbsp (15g)

Procedure

1. Add the figs, raspberries, and chia seeds to a food processor. As smooth as you like, blend.
2. Keep chilled in an airtight jar for at least an hour to thicken.
3. This will last two weeks.

Nutrition per Serving:

Calories – 90 | Fat - 2g | Carbs - 4g | Protein - 2g | Sugar – 0g | Fiber – 1.9g | Potassium - 80mg | Sodium – 60mg | Cholesterol – 0mg

9.11 Mixed hummus

Servings: 10 | Preparation time: 5 mins |
Cooking time: 0 mins

Ingredients

- Cans of chickpeas, 2 (400g tins)
- Peeled garlic cloves, 3.
- Freshly lemon juice, 3tbsp (45g)
- Extra virgin olive oil, 2 tbsp (30g)
- Tahini, 8 tbsp (120g)
- Aquafaba chickpea water, 8tbsp (120g)
- Salt, 1 tsp (5g)
- Cumin, 1tsp (5 g)
- Paprika powder, 1tsp (5 g)

Procedure

1. Drain chickpeas, reserving liquid. In a Thermomix, chop garlic for 5 seconds at speed 8.
2. Add chickpeas, blend until creamy. Adjust seasoning, then serve with a sprinkle of cumin or paprika and a drizzle of oil.

Nutrition per Serving:

Calories – 75 | Fat - 7g | Carbs - 2g | Protein - 2g | Sugar – 1g | Fiber – 0.9g | Potassium - 50mg | Sodium – 236mg | Cholesterol – 0mg

9.12 Plant-based creamy olive

Preparation time: 10 mins |
Cooking time: 1hour | Servings: 16

Ingredients

- White beans, drained, 15.75oz (472g)
- Jarred olives, drained, and divided, 5.75oz (172g)
- Lemon pepper, ½ tsp (2.5g)
- Vegan mayo, two tablespoons (30g)
- Lemon juice, 1 tsp (5g)
- Garlic clove, 1

Procedure

1. Take ten olives out of the drained can. Cut up those ten, then put them aside. The chopped olives will be used as garnish.
2. Check the olives for any errant pits by poking them with a fork or knife. Take out and discard whatever you find.
3. Float the white beans.
4. Peel one garlic clove. There is no need to chop if a high-speed blender is being used. You can include it entirely.
5. Add the drained white beans, drained olives (apart from the 10 you left aside and diced), lemon pepper, mayo, lemon juice, and peeled garlic clove to your high-speed blender.
6. Blend each component until it is smooth and evenly distributed.
7. Place the serving dish with the creamy olive dip within. Garnish with chopped olives and parsley.
8. Refrigerate your olive dip for up to an hour until it is cool enough to serve if it heated up in the blender.

Nutrition per Serving:

Calories – 58 | Fat - 3g | Carbs - 7g | Protein - 2g | Sugar – 1g | Fiber – 1.7g | Potassium - 131mg | Sodium – 170mg | Cholesterol – 0mg

9.13 Mixed sauce

Preparation time: 15 mins |
Cooking time: 0 mins | Servings: 6

Ingredients

- Cilantro, 1 cup chopped (250g)
- Fresh jalapenos, 2
- Garlic cloves, 3
- Raw walnut halves, 1 ¼ cups (sub pumpkin seeds for nut-free), (312g)
- Red pepper flakes, ½ tsp (2.5g)
- Cumin seed ground, ½ tsp (2.5g)
- Cardamom, ½ teaspoon (2.5g)
- Fine sea salt, 1 tsp (5g)
- Fresh lime or lemon juice, 2 tablespoons (30g)
- • Water, 4 tablespoons (60g)

Procedure

1. Remove the seeds from the jalapenos.
2. Slice the jalapenos.
3. In a food processor, combine the sliced jalapenos, garlic cloves, walnuts, cilantro, red pepper flakes, cumin, cardamom, and salt. Process until the mixture forms sticky crumbs.
4. While the food processor is running, gradually add the water until the sauce reaches your desired consistency.
5. Taste the mixture and adjust the seasoning if necessary.
6. Transfer the sauce to a storage container and chill until ready to use.

Nutrition per Serving:

Calories – 142 | Fat - 13g | Carbs - 4g | Protein - 3.5g | Sugar – 1g | Fiber – 1.1g | Potassium - 400mg | Sodium – 315mg | Cholesterol – 0mg

9.14 Vegan sour cream with tofu

Preparation time: 3 mins |
Cooking time: 0 mins | Servings: 10

Ingredients

- Apple cider vinegar, 1 tbsp (15g)
- Silken tofu, 10 oz (300g)
- Salt, ¼ tsp (1.25g)
- Garlic powder, 1 tsp (optional) (5g)
- Chives as a garnish (optional)

Procedure

1. The silken tofu should be drained of any extra liquid.
2. Blend all ingredients in a blender until they are creamy and smooth.
3. Serve alongside your preferred foods.

Nutrition per Serving:

Calories – 20 | Fat - 1g | Carbs - 1g | Protein - 2g | Sugar – 0g | Fiber – 0.3g | Potassium - 70mg | Sodium – 61mg | Cholesterol – 0mg

9.15 Gluten free dip

Preparation time: 5 mins |
Cooking time: 0 mins | Servings: 3

Ingredients

- Olive oil, 3 tablespoons (45g)
- Garlic cloves that have been peeled and lightly mashed with a knife's side, 7.
- Blanched almonds, ½ cup (125g)
- Red bell peppers (about 3 medium peppers), 1 cup (250g)
- Sun-dried tomatoes (about 10–12 halves), 2/3 cup (160g)
- Spanish smoked sweet paprika (Pimenton), 1 tsp (5g)
- Salt, ½ to 1 tsp (season to taste) (2.5g - 5g)

Procedure

1. Olive oil, garlic, and almonds are added to a small skillet that is already heated too medium-high. They should be toasted until golden, and the heat should be distributed evenly by tossing them around the pan. Keep an eye on it because it might turn very quickly.
2. Add them to a food processor with the bell peppers, tomatoes, paprika, salt (start with less and add more if necessary), and 3 to 4 tablespoons of cold water.
3. Blend the ingredients until they are the appropriate consistency. You can keep going until everything is seamless.

Nutrition per Serving:

Calories – 173 | Fat - 4g | Carbs - 2g | Protein - 2g | Sugar – 0g | Fiber – 0.5g | Potassium - 926mg | Sodium – 620mg | Cholesterol – 0mg

10 HOLIDAY BOARDS

10.1 Valentine's charcuterie board

Preparation time: 15 mins |
Cooking time: 0 mins | Servings: 8

Ingredients

- Italian Dry Salami, 1 package 4 oz (113g)
- Grape jam, ½ cup (125g)
- Cherries, ½ cup (95g)
- Blueberries, ½ cup (95g)
- Half-cut strawberries, ½ cup (100g)
- Raspberries, ½ cup (83g)
- Red grapes, ½ cup (125g)
- Herbs and garlic Boursin, 1 box 5 oz (150g)
- Cranberries, ½ cup (95g)
- Wensleydale, Cheese,1 oz (30g)
- Plain goat cheese (colored pink), 8 oz (224g)
- Chocolate truffles, 1 package (108g)
- Conversation Hearts, 1 bag, 6 oz (150g)
- Cinnamon Hearts, 1 bag, 6 oz (150)
- Chocolate hearts, 7 pieces (84g)

Procedure

1. Begin by arranging the cheeses on the charcuterie board in the shape of a heart.
2. Add the salami next. Arrange it like a flower, meaning fan out the slices in a circular pattern. Each slice can represent a 'petal' of the flower, with slices overlapping each other in a radial pattern. This is a decorative technique to enhance the visual appeal of the dish.
3. Add the fruit and grape jam.
4. Cover the remaining space on the board with candy and chocolates.
5. For a nice accent, add some roses

Nutrition per Serving:

Calories – 173| Fat - 5g | Carbs - 28g | Protein - 4g | Sugar – 19g | Fiber – 2.5g | Potassium - 251mg | Sodium – 330mg | Cholesterol – 18mg

10.2 Sweet Romance Charcuterie Board

Preparation time: 10 mins |
Cooking time: 0 mins | Servings: 12

Ingredients

Sauce

- Chocolate sauce, ½ cup (125g)
- Cream of White Chocolate, ½ cup (125g)
- Nutella, ½ cup (125g)

Chocolate

- Chocolates Little Mints are chocolates. 6 bar (49g)
- Chocolate Bark made at home Richardson Link
- Milk Chocolate Oval Shape, 10 bar (80g)
- Assorted Truffles of preference, 10 pieces 30 0z (840g)

Cookies

- Chocolate Cookie tarts with caramel, 10
- Chocolate Almond Wafers
- Milano Chocolate, dark, 6 pieces
- Table Salt as per taste

Fruit

- Raspberries, ½ cup (83g)
- Granadilla Seeds, 1 tbsp (15g)
- Strawberries, ½ cup (95g)

Nuts and pretzels covered in chocolate.

- A little caramel Pretzels, 2 oz (60g)
- Dark and white chocolate-covered pretzels, as well as chocolate-covered almonds, 12g

Procedure

1. Place sauce bowls on a large wooden board. Evenly distribute cookies, pretzels, chocolate-covered almonds, and truffles for variety. In a small bowl, add pomegranate seeds. Fill gaps with strawberries and raspberries.

Nutrition per Serving:

Calories – 26 | Fat - 1g | Carbs - 4g | Protein - 0.4g | Sugar – 3g | Fiber – 1.2g | Potassium - 46mg | Sodium – 1mg | Cholesterol – 3mg

10.3 Charcuterie board for Lover's

Preparation time: 15 mins |
Cooking time: 0 mins | Servings: 12

Ingredients

- Cheeses: 2 oz (60g)
- Blue cheese, 1 oz (30g)
- Cranberry cheese, 2 oz (60g)
- Thinly sliced cheddar cheese, 8 oz (228g)
- Sliced thin genoa salami, 2 oz (60g)
- Prosciutto sliced, 1 oz (20g)
- Orange, sliced 1 cup (250g)
- Red and green grapes, 1 cup (250g)
- Smoked gouda cheese, 2 oz (60g)
- Apricots, dry, ¼ cup (62.5g)
- Green olives, ¼ cup (62.5g)
- Tiny pickles and capers, 1/3 cup (83.3g)
- Almonds, 1 cup (250g)
- Crackers with peach jam and pepper jack, and pita chips.

Procedure

1. Place each component on a dish or cheese board made of wood.
2. Start by randomly placing jars and ramekins.
3. Add the remaining components, distributing them at random so that the sizes and colors are evenly distributed.
4. Dispense and savor!

Nutrition per Serving:

Calories – 163 | Fat - 13g | Carbs - 6g | Protein - 8g | Sugar – 3g | Fiber – 0.9g | Potassium - 154mg | Sodium – 299mg | Cholesterol – 22mg

10.4 Charcuterie board meat for new year eve

Preparation time: 15 mins | Servings: 10

Ingredients

Meat

- Salami dry, 4 oz (112g)

Cheese

- Manchego, 2 oz (60g)
- Garlic and Herbs Bellavitano, 2 oz (60g)
- Herb and Garlic Brie, 2 oz (60g)
- The grapefruit and fig Sheep Cheese, 2 oz (60g)
- Havarti, 2 oz (60g)
- Cheese crackers shaped like letters, 2 oz (60)
- Butter crackers in a circle, 2 oz (60g)

Crackers

- Rectangular crackers for snacks, 2.5 oz (70g)
- Pecan thins, 2oz (60g)
- Butter crackers, 2 oz (60g)

Chocolate

- Rolo-wrapped chocolate, 3 oz (90g)
- Almonds covered with chocolate, 1 oz (30g)

Fruit

- Strawberries, 3 oz (90g)
- Blueberries, 2 oz (60g)
- Raspberries, 3 oz (90g)
- Bunch of grapes , 3 oz (90g)
- Mango, dried, 2 oz (60g)

Pickles and almonds

- Little pickles for snacks, 2 oz (60g)
- Almonds, 2 oz (60g)

Procedure

1. Point the fresh fruit and dried fruit towards the direction of the central bloom. Give the cheese and crackers room to spread out among the fruit.
2. Point the cheese and crackers in the direction of the central blossom. Fill in the blanks so that the options for the fruit, cheese, and crackers alternate. Then utilize the Havarti cheese letter cut outs.
3. Wherever there is empty space on the board, add the chocolate pieces.

4. The pickles and almonds should be used to cover edges and voids.
5. Set up the sparkling cider and disco balls for the visitors on and close to the board.
6. Happy New Year should be displayed in cheesy letters along the top of the board.

Nutrition per Serving:
Calories – 15 | Fat - 0.1g | Carbs - 4g | Protein - 0.3g | Sugar – 2g | Fiber – 0.7g | Potassium - 30mg | Sodium – 0.3mg | Cholesterol – 7mg

10.5 New year charcuterie board

Preparation time: 20 mins |
Cooking time: 0 mins | Servings: 6

Ingredients

- Cupcakes for New Year's Eve, 12 oz (336g)
- Caramel candies and chocolate-covered pretzels, 12 oz (336g)
- Danish biscuits, 10 oz (300g)
- Rock candy in gold, 15 oz (450g)
- Rocky black candy, 15 oz (450g)
- Black gummy bears (1-inch), 6 oz (180g)
- Shiny Gold Gummi Bears (1-inch), 6 oz (180g)
- Miniature black Six lets chocolates, 1 lb (225 pieces) 28g.
- Miniature black Six lets chocolates, 1 lb (28g)
- Miniature chocolates Six lets in shimmering gold, 1 lb. (28g)

Procedure

1. Make sure to choose enough chocolates, cupcakes, and other treats to fill your tray before choosing an attractive board or platter to place your refreshments on.
2. Start by positioning your focal point in the tray's center.
3. Then expand outward from your focal point, arranging the sweets, biscuits, and nibbles in distinctive, enjoyable, and consistent patterns.
4. Provide a few tiny bowls or plates to the tray, position them in an appealing pattern, and then fill with the smaller candies to add visual interest.
5. Fill in any remaining gaps or holes with smaller candies, such as Six lets, to complete the design.
6. Dispense and savor!

Nutrition per Serving:
Calories – 118 | Fat - 5g | Carbs - 18g | Protein - 1g | Sugar – 13g | Fiber – 0.5g | Potassium - 231mg | Sodium – 102mg | Cholesterol – 2mg

10.6 Christmas Cheese Board

Preparation time: 20 mins | Cooking time: 0 mins | Servings: 10

Ingredients

Cheese

- European Camembert, 2 oz (60g)
- Traditional Camembert, 2 oz (60g)
- Slices of diced Provolone and Manchego Gouda, 3 oz (90g)

Meat

- European salami, 3 oz (100g)
- Italian salami, 3 oz (100g)
- Prosciutto, 2 oz (60g)
- Ham slices, 5 oz (150g)
- Salami sticks, 5 oz (150g)

Nuts, fruits, etc.

- Fresh seeds from a pomegranate, 1 tbsp (15g)
- Red currants in season
- Fruit stars, 1 cup (250g)
- Red and green grapes without seeds, 1 cup (250g)
- Kalamata olives, 1 cup (250g)
- Pristine rosemary
- Roasted cashews in honey, 1 cup (250g)
- Fig preserves.
- Cookies with honey, 5 oz (150g)

Procedure

1. Using a star-shaped cookie cutter, create stars out of slices of Provolone cheese. Using the same star-shaped cookie cutter, carve a hole out of one of the Camembert cheese wheels. Pomegranate seeds are then placed within the hole. Star fruit should be cut.
2. Put a collection of miniature salami sticks at the base to serve as the tree trunk. If desired, tie with a string or ribbon to maintain the trunk form.
3. Then place a tree on a rectangle board with a vertical orientation. Build your tree from the base up, starting with a row of red currants.
4. Lines of red and green grapes, cubed gouda, Classic Camembert, and various salami and cheese varieties can then be added. Continue adding layers of ham, prosciutto, olives, salami, and nuts the order is not important; just be inventive and have fun as you arrange the items to resemble a Christmas tree. To ensure the triangle tree shape, make sure each layer of your Christmas tree is just a little bit narrower than the one before it. To simulate pine needles, insert tiny rosemary sprigs between layers.
5. Decorate the tree with star fruit and miniature cheese stars. Use another cheese star, star fruit slice, or festive star-shaped cookie as the garnish at the top.
6. Place any sweets, spreads, or dips around your board last. Also add crackers, bread, and biscotti.

Nutrition per Serving:

Calories – 442 | Fat - 35g | Carbs - 120g | Protein - 60g | Sugar – 12g | Fiber – 4g | Potassium - 400mg | Sodium – 130mg | Cholesterol – 42mg

10.7 Charcuterie boards for Christmas

Preparation time: 20 mins | Cooking time: 0 mins | Servings: 10

Ingredients

Regarding the Caprese Tree

- Fresh spinach, stems removed, 2 cups (500g)
- Cherry tomatoes, 10.5 oz (315g)
- Small or one large jar of fresh basil, 2-3
- Mozzarella balls, 8 oz (240g)

For the Time Being

- Fresh mozzarella, 8 ounces (240g)
- Garlic and basil.

Regarding the balsamic glaze

- Balsamic vinegar, half a cup (125g)
- Dried cranberries are all around.1/2 cup (125g)

Leading right corner

- Grape vines, 1 oz (30g)
- Slice of brie, 1 oz (30 g)

Highest left corner

- High-quality firm salami, 1-6 oz (30-180g)
- Nuts mixed, 1 cup (250g)

Right Side

- Asparagus bunch, 1 oz (30g)
- Prosciutto package, 6 oz (180g)

Procedure

For the tree

1. On the cheese board, draw the contour of the tree with entire pieces of spinach that have had their stems removed. Remember that the star will be on the very top branch, therefore space the spinach leaves apart to make the tree grow downward.
2. Calculate the length of the skewers using the outline.
3. To maintain balance, alternate the mozzarella, basil, tomato, basil, and mozzarella such that whatever was at the beginning of the skewer is also at the finish. The second row should then be on a 4 inch skewer. Starting with a tomato this time. Start with 4 on a skewer for the third row, and then gauge how many toothpicks you'll need by placing one on the spinach.
4. Once the skewer is full, insert the toothpick into the end and continue until the desired length is reached.

For the presents

1. Lay the Triscuits out to create the presents under the tree. For a couple of the "gifts," construct a bow out of thinly sliced fresh mozzarella.
2. For the tree's top, cut a star from the fresh mozzarella log using a star cutter.

Vinegar Glaze

1. Balsamic vinegar and honey are combined, and they are simmered for 20 minutes while occasionally stirred until reduced.
2. Put a small serving bowl with dried cranberries around it after pouring it in.

Corner on the right

Slice a brie wedge and place it. Put a grape vine next to it.

Corner on the left

Place the nuts in a festive bowl in the left corner and enclose it with salami.

For the Baked Asparagus with Prosciutto

1. Prosciutto slices should be cut in half lengthwise. Put them on a baking sheet with parchment paper after tightly wrapping them around an asparagus spear that has been cut. Olive oil should be poured over them before baking for 10 minutes at 400 degree Fahrenheit (204 degree Celsius).
2. Before placing them on your board, take them out of the oven and set them on a roasting rack so that any excess fat may drop out.

Nutrition per Serving:

Calories: 615 | Fat: 39g | Carbohydrates: 44g | Protein: 25g | Sugar: 11g | Fiber: 3g | Potassium: 295mg | Sodium: 925mg | Cholesterol: 25mg

10.8 Mini charcuterie board

Preparation time: 15 mins |
Cooking time: 0 mins | Servings: 6

Ingredients

- Meats, 6 oz (180g)
- Turkey pepperoni, 5 oz (150g)
- Summer sausage, 7 oz (210g)
- Bourson cheese, 5 oz (150g)
- Cheddar cheese, 7 ounces (210g)
- Brie cheese, 8 oz (240g)
- Blue cheese, 5 ounces (150g)
- Sliced from 1 big baguette.
- Any crackers, 1 packet 3 oz (100g)
- Dried apricots, 8 oz (240g)
- Among the ingredients in your cupboard are honey, pesto, olives, pretzels, nuts, fancy mustard, marmalade, fresh fruits, and veggies.

Procedure

1. Place the ingredients that are now in bowls on your board in various locations to begin.
2. Place the softer cheeses, such as brie, bleu cheese, and Boursin cheese, on the wooden board in an attractive arrangement.
3. Around the board, arrange the meats.
4. Crackers and sliced baguette are then added.
5. Dried and/or fresh fruits, almonds, pretzels, and other snacks, start to fill in the gaps.
6. Small pieces of cheese, nuts, or other dried fruits can be used to fill up any gaps. Make a glass of wine for yourself and unwind!

Nutrition per Serving:

Calories: 617 | Fat: 40g | Carbohydrates: 30g | Protein: 90g | Sugar: 2g | Fiber: 5g | Potassium: 350mg | Sodium: 120mg | Cholesterol: 40mg

10.9 Easy Charcuterie board recipe

Preparation time: 15 mins |
Cooking time: 0 mins | Servings: 7

Ingredients

- Parmesan Reggiano cheese, 2 oz (60g)
- Meat and seafood, 1-2 pieces 3 oz (100g)
- Crackers, pretzels, popcorn, sliced bread, or crostini, 1-3 pieces 3 oz (100g)
- Jam, jelly, sauce, dip, or honey, 2 tbsp each (30g)
- Mixed nuts, ½ cup (125g)
- Any fresh fruit, 1 piece 1 oz (30g)
- Any dried fruit, 1 oz (30g)
- Artichokes, grilled or marinated, 1-2

Procedure

1. Any bowl should go first. Place any larger blocks of cheese or other bulky things behind that (salami rose or smoked salmon piece). This establishes your framework. After that, you should arrange your objects in descending order, paying particular attention to the next largest or heaviest items. The gaps should be filled in and the objects should gradually get smaller.
2. Stir up activity on the board.
3. To make a beautiful board, you want to make use of movement. Try different locations on the board for your bowls to be placed off-center. You can arrange the meals in a combination of flowing designs or more straight lines. Play freely and without fear.

Compare your colors.

1. Contrast your colors when you arrange your dishes on the board in various spots.
2. If you have white crackers, for instance, you might put them alongside green or red grapes rather than white cheese. This generates exciting visuals.

Change up your sizes and cutting methods.

3. Try different combinations of bigger and smaller objects. Additionally, you can experiment with different cutting sizes. For a striking contrast, you could,

for instance, cut several slices from one block of cheese and place them next to the other block. A salami stick could be used in a similar manner.

4. You can also play around with other cutting patterns. You can use interesting crisscross or dragon cuts, or you can cut items in a primitive fashion. You can arrange meats in rose shapes.

Nutrition per Serving:

Calories: 320 | Fat: 12g | Carbohydrates: 4g | Protein: 1g | Sugar: 1g | Fiber: 2g | Potassium: 24mg | Sodium: 144mg | Cholesterol: 10mg

10.10 Charcuterie cups

Preparation time: 25 mins | Cooking time: 0 mins | Servings: 10

Ingredients

- Crackers, 3 oz (100g)
- Salami, 12 slices or pepperoni 4 oz (120g)
- Turkey or Ham, 12 slices 3 oz (90g)
- Thick Cut Cheddar Cheese, 12 slices, 3 oz (90g)
- Havarti Cheese, 12 slices, 3 oz (90g)
- Asiago cheese, 24 cubes 5 oz (150g)
- Grapes, 60 pieces 1 cup (250g)
- Thinly sliced tiny Fuji apple, 1 1 oz (30g)
- Whole black olives, 1 cup (250g)
- Baby carrots, 1 cup (250g)
- Nuts, seeds, and dried fruit. 1 ½ cup (375g)

Procedure

1. After preparing everything, you can start filling the cups. Add 2 tablespoons of nuts, seeds, or dried fruit, 2 pieces of meat, 2-3 crackers, 4-6 pieces of cheese, 5 grapes, berries, or slices of fruit, plus a few extras like a tiny carrot and black olives, depending on the size of your cup. In order to conserve space and improve the appearance of the Charcuterie Cups, also roll, or fold the meat. The aforementioned components are intended to be distributed equally among 12 cups.
2. Large toothpicks are another addition It is used to hold cheese balls, black olives, and miniature pickles. This makes it easier to segregate things and keeps everything organized. The preparation will mostly depend on the components you wish to use and the preferences of your visitors. This is only a general outline, so feel free to add additional details if you like.

Nutrition per Serving:

Calories: 517 | Fat: 38g | Carbohydrates: 20g | Protein: 26.1g | Sugar: 5.9g | Fiber: 4g | Potassium: 336mg | Sodium: 1216mg | Cholesterol: 30mg

10.11 Delicious baked brie

Preparation time: 10 mins |
Cooking time: 8 mins | Servings: 8

Ingredients

- Brie, 8 oz (240g)
- Prepared basil pesto, 2 tsp (10g)
- Roasting 1/4 cup of garlic cloves (62g)
- Flake red pepper with a pinch.
- Toasted bread or crackers for serving 3 oz (100g)

Procedure

1. Turn on the oven and Set the temperature to 350 degrees Fahrenheit (176.6 degree Celsius). The brie should be placed on a rimmed baking pan lined with baking parchment paper and lightly crisscrossed with a sharp knife.
2. Brie should be baked for 10 to 12 minutes, or until the middle is softened but the outside is still firm.
3. Transfer the bribe to a serving tray with care and top with the pesto, garlic, and red pepper flakes. Serve right away with bread or crackers.

Nutrition per Serving:

Calories: 126 | Fat: 10g | Carbohydrates: 2g | Protein: 7g | Sugar: 0g | Fiber: 0g | Potassium: 519mg | Sodium: 217mg | Cholesterol: 28mg

10.12 Christmas wreath charcuterie board

Preparation time: 15 mins |
Cooking time: 0 mins | Servings: 10

Ingredients

- Spinach, 3 oz (90g)
- Cherry tomatoes, 1 cup (250g)
- Feta cheese squares, 2 oz (60g)
- Skewers of pickled vegetables, 1 cup (250g)
- Slices of salami, 3 oz (90g)
- Macadamia nuts, 1 oz (30g)

Procedure

1. Start assembling the charcuterie board's foundation for your Christmas wreath. The spinach will be used to create a circle around the edge of your board or dish.
2. Distribute the pickled veggie skewers and cherry tomatoes on the board.
3. In the spaces between the tomatoes and the pickled vegetable skewers, sprinkle the chopped feta cheese and macadamia nuts over the spinach circle.
4. The hardest part of making your salami roses will probably be the shaping. Utilize a glass that is appropriate for your round meat slices.
5. Put a slice of beef on the glass' rim. Fold into and out of the glass by half.
6. When there is no more room inside the glass, keep going, overlapping slices all around the rim. To make the salami roses, eight pieces ought to be sufficient. In case the rose begins to emerge before you have finished placing it on the board, place your palm close to the top of the glass. Turning the glass upside-down and placing the salami rose on your board will do this.

Nutrition per Serving:

Calories – 501 | Fat - 40g | Carbs - 11g | Protein - 25g | Sugar – 7g | Fiber – 2g | Potassium - 760mg | Sodium – 1660mg | Cholesterol – 30mg

10.13 Cocktails board with orange

Preparation time: 15 mins | Cooking time: 0 mins | Servings: 6

Ingredients

Basic Syrup

- Granulated Sugar, 2 cups (500g)
- Water, 2 cups (500g)

Cocktails

- Ice
- Gin Syrup, 2 oz (60g)
- Orange Juice, 2 oz (60g)
- Riondo Champagne, 3 oz (100ml)
- Orange peels, either candied or fresh

Procedure

Basic Syrup

1. In a large glass measuring cup, mix the water and sugar.
2. Stirring in between each minute of microwaving will help the sugar dissolve. Before using, let the food in the refrigerator cool completely for at least 6 hours.
3. This amount provides food for a modest gathering. According to your demands, increase or decrease the amounts.

Cocktails

1. Add ice to the cocktail shaker. Add the orange juice, simple syrup, and gin. Shake the ingredients for 20 seconds to blend and refrigerate it.
2. Fill 2 glasses with the juice mixture.
3. Pour champagne on top. Serve with orange peel as a garnish.

Nutrition per Serving:

Calories – 140 | Fat - 5g | Carbs - 30g | Protein - 2g | Sugar – 2g | Fiber – 0.5g | Potassium - 340mg | Sodium – 120mg | Cholesterol – 0mg

10.14 Platter of holiday

Preparation time: 15 mins | Cooking time: 0 mins | Servings: 10

Ingredients

- Pepperoncini, 3 oz (90g)
- Savory cherry peppers, 2 oz (60g)
- Kalamata olives with marinated artichokes, 2 oz (60g)
- Mozzarella bocconcini, 3 oz (90g)
- Provolone cheese chunked, 2 oz (60g)
- Thinly sliced Italian dry salami made with prosciutto, 3 oz (90g)
- For garnish, use fresh rosemary.

Procedure

1. Arrange the meat in the center of a circular plate or platter. The cheese should then be placed around the meat, with olives added for texture. Last but not least, arrange the artichokes and peppers in a ring around the cheese. As a garnish, tuck the rosemary into the platter's border.
2. Enjoy the season of giving!

Nutrition per Serving:

Calories – 210 | Fat - 2g | Carbs - 14g | Protein - 4g | Sugar – 5g | Fiber – 1.5g | Potassium - 1067mg | Sodium – 1214mg | Cholesterol – 15mg

10.15 Savore Christmas board

Preparation time: 20 mins |
Cooking time: 0 mins | Servings: 8

Ingredients

- Fresh foliage, such as curly kale, rosemary, or eucalyptus sprigs, ½ cup (125g)
- Cheddar cheese cubed, 7 oz (210g)
- Pepper jack cheese cubed, 7 oz (210g)
- Colby cheese cubed, 8 oz (240g)
- Fresh mozzarella balls, 7 ounces (210g)
- Halved cherry tomatoes, 1 cup (250g)
- Cured and pitted black olives, 1 cup (250g)
- Cured and pitted green olives, 1 cup (250g)
- Sliced pepperoni, 7 oz (210g)
- Sliced salami, 8 oz (240g)
- Green, seedless grapes 7 ounces (210g)

Procedure

1. Start by placing one of the four varieties of cheese in each corner of the wreath.
2. When adding the tomatoes, grapes, and olives, keep in mind the layout as you arrange piles of each component.
3. Lastly, add the meat. We do this because the other ingredients will assist keep the meat erect and the pepperoni and salami will be arranged in wonderful fluffy configurations. The sliced meats can either be folded into rosettes, or you can simply place each piece amid the other ingredients by folding it in half twice.
4. Make sure your wreath is spherical and gently reposition any components that aren't exactly where they belong. Then, using your greenery, adorn the circle's perimeter and interior. Serve crackers or snacks alongside your charcuterie.

Nutrition per Serving:

Calories – 210 | Fat - 30g | Carbs - 20g | Protein - 12g | Sugar – 7g | Fiber – 2.5g | Potassium - 690mg | Sodium – 380mg | Cholesterol – 35mg

11 ALPHABETICAL INDEX

12 CONCLUSION

As you close the pages of "Charcuterie Board Cookbook," you are not merely ending a culinary journey; you are stepping forward as a master of the artful spread. Each recipe has been carefully crafted to transform your gatherings into a symphony of flavors and a mosaic of textures. From the lush valleys of cheese pairings to the peaks of perfectly cured meats, you've traversed a landscape of tastes that elevate the simple act of eating into a communal celebration.

With your newfound skills, every board you present will tell its own tale—one of care, creativity, and conviviality. Your tables will no longer be just surfaces for dining but canvases for creation. So, as you set forth, remember that each slice, each placement, each pairing, is a reflection of your passion and the timeless tradition of sharing. May your boards brim with abundance and your gatherings echo with laughter and delight. Bon appétit!

13 BONUS

BONUS: Scanning the following QR code will take you to a web page where you can access 9 fantastic bonuses after leaving your email and an honest review of my book on Amazon: 7 online courses about charcuterie board basics and compositions and 2 mobile apps about charcuterie board basics and arrangements and recipes.
Link: https://dl.bookfunnel.com/ggwomfciji

14 ANNEX A

STORAGE AND REHEATING

LEFTOVER FOOD	REFRIGERATION TIME	FREEZING TIME	SPECIAL INSTRUCTIONS
PASTA, RICE AND GRAINS	3-5 days	3 months	Store in air-tight containers to avoid moisture build-up; may require reheating with a splash of water.
VEGATBLES	3-4 days	1-2 months	Blanch before freezing to preserve
FRUITS	5-7 days (if cut)	2-6 months	Can become soft; store without cutting for best quality.
SALADS	3-5 days	Not Recommended	Don't freeze due to wilting and high moisture content.
SEAFOOD	1-2 days	3-6 months	Pack tightly; risk of freezer burn
MEAT	3-4 days	2-6 months	Avoid freezer burn by sealing tightly; flavor may diminish over extended time.
DAIRY ITEMS	1-2 days	1-2 months	Can experience separation or curdling; best used in cooked dishes after freezing.
SMOOTHIES	1-2 days	4-6 months	Store fruits and other ingredients in zip-lock bags to avoid moisture and items getting rotten
BAKED ITEMS	3-7 days	2-3 months	Allow to cool completely before freezing; frosting or fillings may change in texture.
SOUPS AND STEWS	3-4 days	4-6 months	Cool before freezing; might require mixing after thawing due to possible separation.

***NOTE:** Best tip to store food items is to make divide your meals into smaller portion sizes that can be consumed at a single time. Place each portion in an air tight zip-lock bags. This tip might help support better freezing in order to avoid repeated reheating and save the nutritional content of foods.

15 ANNEX B

WASHING AND HANDLING

Importance of Proper Cleaning

Before delving into the intricacies of plant-based cooking, it's crucial to understand the importance of thoroughly washing fruits and vegetables. Doing so removes dirt, bacteria, and any pesticide residues, ensuring that your dishes are not only delicious but also safe to eat.

Step-by-Step Guide to Washing Produce

1. **Hand Hygiene:** First and foremost, before and after you prepare any fruits or vegetables, wash your hands thoroughly for at least 15-20 seconds using warm water and hand soap. This crucial step minimizes the transfer of bacteria to your food.
2. **Prepare Vinegar and Salt Solution:** Combine 1 1/3 cup of vinegar and 1 tablespoon of salt in a large bowl. Stir the mixture until both the vinegar and salt have completely dissolved. The vinegar serves as a natural disinfectant, while the salt aids in drawing out hidden microbes.
3. **Initial Rinse:** Fruits and vegetables should be initially rinsed under running water. It's essential to gently rub the surface to loosen dirt and any lingering pesticides. Avoid using soap or chemical cleansers as these can leave residues that are harmful if ingested.
4. **Soaking:** Different types of produce require different soaking times. For thin-skinned fruits and vegetables like berries and leafy greens, a 5-minute soak in the vinegar and salt solution is sufficient. Firm-skinned produce like apples and squash should be left in the solution for about 10 minutes. This step is critical for thorough disinfection.
5. **Scrubbing:** For hard and textured fruits or vegetables like melons, carrots, sweet potatoes, and cucumbers, utilize a clean vegetable brush to scrub their skins gently. This removes trapped dirt and microbes that a simple rinse may not eliminate.
6. **Rinsing Post-Soak:** After soaking and scrubbing, rinse the produce under running plain water to remove any lingering vinegar or salt. Make sure to rinse thoroughly to ensure that no residues are left behind.
7. **Drying:** Use a clean kitchen cloth or paper towel to dry the fruits and vegetables. This step is more than just for convenience; it further minimizes the chance of bacterial growth.
8. **Inspect and Cut:** Finally, inspect your produce for any damaged or bruised areas. Cut these away as they can harbor bacteria and negatively affect the quality and safety of your food. Designate separate cutting boards for fruits/vegetables and raw meats. Always wash boards with hot soapy water after use.
9. **Meat:** Wash hands, meat, and utensils with soap and hot water to prevent cross-contamination, then pat meat dry before seasoning or cooking. Follow proper cooking temperatures and times to ensure meat is safely prepared and cooked to the recommended internal temperature.

Extra Tips

- Leafy Greens: For leafy greens like kale and spinach, a salad spinner can be incredibly useful to remove excess water post-washing.
- Berry Care: Berries are delicate. Rinse them only before you're about to use them to prevent spoilage.
- Storing: Some fruits and vegetables like tomatoes and avocados should be stored at room temperature until they ripen; then, they can be refrigerated.

Remember, clean produce contributes to safe and delicious meals!

16 MEASUREMENT CHART

Volume Equivalents (Dry)	
US STANDARD	**METRIC**
1/8 teaspoon	0.5 ml
1/4 teaspoon	1 ml
1/2 teaspoon	2 ml
3/4 teaspoon	4 ml
1 teaspoon	5 ml
1 tablespoon	15 ml
1/4 cup	59 ml
1/2 cup	118 ml
3/4 cup	177 ml
1 cup	235 ml
2 cups	475 ml
3 cups	700 ml
4 cups	1 L

Volume Equivalents (Liquid)		
US STANDARD	**US STANDARD (OUNCES)**	**METRIC (APPROX.)**
2 tablespoons	1 fl. oz.	30 ml
1/4 cup	2 fl. oz.	60 ml
1/2 cup	4 fl. oz.	120 ml
1 cup	8 fl. oz.	240 ml
1 1/2 cup	12 fl. oz.	355 ml
2 cups or 1 pint	16 fl. oz.	475 ml
4 cups or 1 quart	32 fl. oz.	1 L
1 gallon	128 fl. oz.	4 L

Temperature Equivalents	
FAHR.(F)	**METRIC**
225 °F	107 °C
250 °F	120 °C
275 °F	135 °C
300 °F	150 °C
325 °F	160 °C
350 °F	180 °C
375 °F	190 °C
400 °F	205 °C
425 °F	220 °C
450 °F	235 °C
475 °F	245 °C

Weight Equivalents	
US STANDARD	**METRIC (APPROXIMATE)**
1 ounce	28 g
2 ounces	57 g
5 ounces	142 g
10 ounces	284 g
15 ounces	425 g
16 ounces (1 pound)	455 g
1.5 pounds	680 g
2 pounds	907 g

Milton Keynes UK
Ingram Content Group UK Ltd.
UKHW051218151223
434437UK00016B/616